Release Your Inner Queen of Sheba!

Procedure and Protocols to lead your best life

Release Your Inner Queen of Sheba!

Procedure and Protocols
to lead your best life

Heba Alshareef

Hassay House

Hassay House Inc.
www.hassayhouse.com

Printed in the United States of America
First Edition Printing: December 2008

Cataloging-in-Publication Data
Alshareef, Heba
     Release your inner queen of Sheba–procedure and protocols to lead your
     best life/Heba Alshareef
     p. cm.
     ISBN 978-0-9811560-0-2

    1.   Adult – Conduct of life. 2. Heba Alshareef I. Title: Release your
        inner queen of Sheba – procedure and protocols to lead your best
        life. II. Title.

0-9811560

Who would a queen be without her supporters?
To my family,
and especially my king

$\mathcal{C}$ontents

If you could be a queen, which one would you be?

By way of Introduction

Cinderella had it going on. For years she was the end all, be all, idol for millions of girls around the world - Muslim girls included. In fact, despite her recent foray into the world of women's rights in recent twists on the classic, she still is. Recently, I was talking to my fourteen-year-old niece about the importance of working hard in school, how being educated could only make her stronger, and she responded that school didn't matter much. She had decided that she was going to marry rich, someone who would treat her like a princess and hire servants to take care of her every whim. Her Prince Charming would be dashing, sweep her off her feet, jet her to Paris for croissants and café au lait one week, take her on a private tour of the Taj Mahal the next. She wouldn't have to work, wouldn't have to worry, and wouldn't have to want. She would be Cinderella.

Try as I might to convince her that Cinderella is a fictional character with an even more fictional tale, my niece, suffering from the hearing impairment that ails the common teenager, just wouldn't listen. Her mother shrugged and made a comment under her breath that only the adults in the room could hear, and only the female ones could understand: *"she'll find out soon enough."*

Soon enough, indeed.

How many girls have grown up with this ideal only to be shocked at the reality that is life? Are you a Cinderella wannabe? Were you a Cinderella wannabe? If not, you're in the minority. I know I definitely was, and my husband of over 15 years might argue that I still am.

But I've found something better.

I had been writing for awhile, teaching for awhile, and having a few children for awhile, when I decided to formalize my addiction to personal growth principles (I had read what seemed like all the books on the subject) and train in NLP and life coaching. One day, while teaching the methodology of dynamic public speaking, the class was asked to reword typical, supposedly meant to be inspirational, lectures that happen in communities across the world. The first one was called 'Female Role Models.' In a flash, my arm shot up. I instantly knew the answer, *the answer*. The trainer, catching the speed of it, remarked, "Heba, you have the best answer in the class."

"Release Your Inner Queen of Sheba!"
You better believe it was the best answer!

Over the months this concept has evolved into something that I never could have anticipated during that second of inspiration. By the mercy of Allah, the entire coaching practice I've established has been about getting the women I work with to release their own inner queen of Sheba.

The idea behind the concept is that we, as Muslim women, have a legacy of strength that we can look upon and go back to when life teaches us that it's not all a fairytale with princes, servants, and castles. When we're struck with the reality of finishing school, having to pay the bills, bad choices, or a husband who refuses to put his socks

where they're supposed to go, we can learn to stay true. When we're brought down by the lack of goal setting, the tragedies that happen to us or our loved ones, the anger, the stress, the guilt, and the sadness that plagues us at odd hours of our day, we can learn to stay true.

We can learn to stay true to our heritage and become strong Muslim women who lead their lives with abundance. How do we do this? We do this by releasing our inner queen of Sheba. We do this by living our best destinies, by moving towards what Allah wants for us, by finding what will bring us happiness right *now*.

And a funny thing happens when we learn to release our inner queens of Sheba. We become stronger, better women who are able to weather the storms and able to actually get our 'happily ever after.' Trust me when I say, Cinderella has nothing on the queen of Sheba!

Maybe you've been a queen of Sheba all your life, maybe you're just starting to be her, or maybe you feel like you'll always be nothing better than someone who reads her tale and takes nothing from it. Whatever your current situation, you now hold in your hands the tools that, by the grace and mercy of Allah, should inspire you to be accountable to yourself and to what you know you can do and who you can be.

My aim is not to turn this into a discussion about the rights of women in Islam, but to enlighten today's Muslim women with the knowledge and the action plans to become someone who knows herself and knows her rights.
She'll learn that the process of harnessing her best self will bring her joy with balance and piece of mind.

It's all a journey, and today you hold in your hands the work of my journey. One year ago, I had no clue what this whole queen of Sheba thing would mean, but somehow, I always knew there would be a book. You see, writing it was always inherit to what I've wanted to do, a perfect match for my vision.

Later, you'll hear more about the vision part; in the

meantime, I'd like to get yourself something to record your thoughts in. It could be a treasured journal with flowers and pink lace, or it could be scraps of recycled paper. Whatever works best for you is what will work best for you. Remember that one. *Whatever works best for you is what will work best for you.*

Did you write it down? You are a quick study!

Who is the queen of Sheba and what does she have to do with me?

The legendary queen finds herself a heroine in many faiths and traditions. As I researched her history for the purpose of this book, I found that much of what is said is almost mythical in nature. I won't discuss the details (although it actually makes for some pretty interesting reading) but suffice it to say that for a woman to inspire so many versions of her tale and presence is phenomenal. In Judeo-Christian traditions, she is the same queen of Sheba mentioned in the Quran, and because the Quran is the final revelation, what I learn about her from there is what I use in this book.

In the Quran and the meanings of the verses in which she appears, she is Bilqis the queen of (to use the Arabic name) Saba. Most historians agree that the region is known in our modern age as Yemen. In the Quran, the queen is introduced to us through the story of the Prophet Solomon, peace be upon him. Solomon, the son of the Prophet David (he who had slain Goliath), is known for his wisdom. He prays to Allah to grant him a kingdom, the likes of which will never be seen after him. His prayers are answered and to Solomon belonged sway over the winds, the command of an army that included jinn and animals (of which he could understand their languages) and close access to Allah. (Quran 38: 30-40)

It is likely that Solomon was the most powerful man who

ever lived. Thus it is that the stage is set for Bilqis, and you know what they say about every great man having a great woman behind him. Although the exact nature of their relationship hasn't been completely authenticated, as we go along we'll be referring to the story as mentioned in the Quran – especially as it pertains to the process outlined in releasing your own inner queen of Sheba.

We'll also be looking to such great women as whom we are privy to be the descendants of on this earth. We can learn to be inspired by exemplary women like Khadijah and Aisha, may Allah be pleased with them, who were the noble and strong wives of the Prophet Muhammad, peace be upon him, and who are, till this very day, our mothers.

You will find that beginning to live your best life is something that you can and must do, that being strong and happy while still fulfilling your duties is inherit to who you are. It is not something that you have to struggle with or feel like you are destined to fail. Yes, you can be the ideal daughter, mother, wife, and friend. Yes, you can be the savvy businesswoman, the conscientious student, and the committed volunteer. And no, it's not a mold that you have to squeeze yourself into. The role is yours. The standard is yours. You are the queen.

With a solid plan of action, as outlined in this book and the incentive to live up to your destiny as a daughter of great women, you have in your hearts and in your hands, and through your reliance on your Lord, the power to shine, to excel, and to be happy. That is what releasing your inner queen of Sheba can do for you.

A word of caution

Before we go any further, let me just say that this book is not a discourse on the rights of women in Islam. Even though the issue of women's rights in Islam is a hot topic, it isn't my desire to get embroiled in the discussion. Let me just say here that releasing your inner queen of Sheba is about finding *your* best self, and it has nothing to do with ascribing to a certain political or socio-economic group of women either. This isn't about feminism or the need to establish it for Muslim women. This isn't about organizing a group to fight for equality for women. This isn't about bringing down the men.

This is about you. And if the 'you' that you discover through this process is the one fighting for equality for others, then that is about *you*. Or if the 'you' that you discover through this process is the one who decides that she is going to embrace the role of the obedient wife, then that is about *you* to. This is about YOU. Unless, "you" happens to be someone mentioned by name in the story, then this isn't about *you*.*

If you have ever questioned yourself or wondered what you are capable of, but been at a loss for a response, know that all the answers are within you. Your strength lies in your ability to listen and heed and comprehend this strength. Your strength lies in your dedication to living your life in a way that is well planned out, set with goals and a higher purpose. Your strength lies in recognizing and appreciating the favors that Allah has bestowed upon you and allowing that to propel you into a lifetime of happiness and inner peace. It is my hope and prayer that through finding your strength, you will live your life full of hope, happiness, and the desire to continually progress in a way that is pleasing to your Creator.

It's like that. Bottom line.

So, let us begin. It's time to discover the kind of queen you are meant to be. Oh, and if you happen to know Cinderella you might want to get her a copy of the book.

Heba Alshareef

*All names have been changed to protect the privacy of the individuals - and if you think you recognize yourself in any of the scenarios presented in the book, but I haven't spoken to you about it beforehand, then rest assured, it's not you. I'm continually amazed at how similar our stories are, how alike are our struggles. I might write something and have ten different women ask if they were the inspiration behind it, if I had been referring to them in it. I tell them what I'm saying here. I know this footnote is getting long, but I just want to make it clear that it is about you, but she (of any specific scenario) isn't you...specifically. We good? Good.

Part One

Solomon, after building the Dome of the Rock in the city of Jerusalem, sets out on travels that will allow him to gain knowledge, spread the religion of Allah, and take lessons from the advanced irrigation systems of far off places. Deciding he wants to implement such irrigation systems close to home, he gathers his workers, a host of men, jinn, and animals, so that they can get started on the project. Solomon is furious when he sees that a particular hoopoe bird, (whom he's sent out to survey the land for underground water sources) is missing.

The hoopoe bird finally appears and cries foul! He has a good excuse for his tardiness. He has come across a queen who has a grand throne. She's so well-off and influential, but she, along with her people, has turned away from the favors of Allah, and is worshipping the sun instead. Solomon reacts to this news by sending the hoopoe bird back with a letter addressed to the queen of Sheba. Solomon, peace be upon him, instructs the bird to watch the scene unfold and to report back to him on what the queen does.

What will she do? We'll revisit the tale of Bilqis as the story of how we can release our own inner queen of

Sheba unfolds, but in the meantime, let's look at this first part and see how it manifests itself here.

Solomon's letter is meant to test her, to see who Bilqis is and how she will react. And this is precisely the objective of part one of the book. In this part, the plan is to start getting to know yourself in ways you probably never understood. What truly motivates you? What are your values? What thoughts do you have about yourself? And, more importantly, are they working to your advantage?

In the next few chapters, you'll learn the first component of releasing your inner queen of Sheba; how to get in touch with your most authentic self. You'll learn what inspires you. You'll learn the absolute habits you must foster in order to move forward (and how to nourish them).

You'll do this is by following the protocols at the end of each chapter. These protocols are specially designed to build upon each other so that you can easily understand and exercise your potential in 21 steps or protocols. In the first 7, you'll realize that what works for you *is* what will work best for you.

1

Will the real

queen of Sheba

please stand up?

It's my life! This statement, usually yelled in frustration when someone has reached a point where the interference of others has infuriated them enough to start staking a claim on something that, alas, they may already feel is spinning out of their control.

To the outside world, Sarah might have seemed like she had it all. She's smart and beautiful, the daughter of wildly successful and beautiful people. Sarah was on her way to finishing medical school, when she married an accomplished doctor. But, when I met her, things were different. She was in the midst of a divorce, had dropped out of medical school with a year left, moved in with her brother and his family of five, and taken a job as an administrative assistant in a bookkeeping company.

And, she adamantly insists, she's never been happier.

"It's not that I enjoy the mechanical and, I'll admit it, 'menial' tasks of this job, but I'm grateful for it because it's allowing me to make the most of this transitional phase. I have a plan for my life, and for the first time, I actually believe that I can do what I want. I'm excited for my future!" she exclaims, and her enthusiasm is contagious.

She says that she knows that others might not understand it, but she's happy that she was able to decipher what she wanted for her life before she hit thirty.

"If I were to follow my mother's example," she laments, "I might still be waiting for clarity."

According to Sarah, her mother was a 'zombie', a woman who had tolerated a lifetime of unhappiness with a husband who was driven by money, and entertained by bullying his family. When her new husband started exhibiting the same behaviors, Sarah stepped back and wondered if the problem was him, or if there was something wrong with her? She saw herself repeating her mother's reactions to certain situations and she realized that she'd been going through the motions of her own life in typical 'zombie' fashion. And it's not to say that all this happened in one spectacular, life-altering, 'AHA' moment, because it didn't. Plus, she didn't have access to this book, as it hadn't been written yet.

In fact, the change was one that was building up, as it builds up in so many of those who belong to the 'outside world'. When people aren't happy, they *look for* change. When people recognize their faults and bad habits, they *try* to make some changes. When people feel like they are failing, they *give up*. Notice the words in italics: look for, try, and give up. All three equate to zero action taken. So, what made Sarah different from others?

She simply started *walking* the walk in her own life. Did she make the right decisions? I don't know. Will she forever be happy? I don't know that either. But having knowledge of the future is not the point. The point is that it is her life, and she's *choosing* to be an active participant in it. She's *doing* what needs to be done in order to get clarity for herself at this precise moment. Notice the words in italics: walking, choosing, doing. Aren't action verbs exciting?

Sarah is an extreme example, and you don't have to forsake all that you've ever known to feel like you are moving ahead and taking action. But, you do have to start exploring the idea of who you are. You have to know yourself, because having clarity on what makes you tick means knowledge, and knowledge will always mean power.

Intimately comprehending who you are and what factors motivate you are the first steps in releasing your inner queen of Sheba. To do this, you'll likely have to go through a metamorphosis. And just like the caterpillar must first shed its skin to become the butterfly, so must we strip the layers around our hearts - the layers that have hidden our potential and blocked us from the beauty of our identities.

Sometimes, this first step of metamorphosis is as simple as realizing we need a change. Other times, it can be forced on us through no fault of our own (or perhaps a fault of our own - realizing this is also part of the process). Perhaps it's a time of transition in your life that forces you to look at yourself in a new light. Perhaps you've been hurt badly by someone. Perhaps you've embraced a new role; gotten married, or become a mother. Whatever the case may be, you're in a great position to start becoming the best you, to start spreading your wings as that beautiful butterfly.

As scary as it sounds to 'shed your skin,' I would say that the first step to stripping away the layers and seen what lies beneath can be a very soothing and comforting experience. It is what you make of it. And since you are in queen mode, how about pampering yourself as you begin?

Protocol 1

Please have ready your journal, a pen, and a soothing cup of your favorite herbal tea. Dedicate a time (if you have children, it might have to be in the wee hours of the early morning) when you can completely focus on you.

At the top of page 1, write down: ***Who am I?***

Proceed to answer this question. There are no wrong answers and no limit on what you write down or how little space the answer takes in your journal, or how much. And take as long as you need, I'll be waiting on you.

The answers may come automatically to you. It may have been a process whereby you answered the question by defining who you are NOT. Or perhaps it is that the answer has you feeling vulnerable, because you've brought down the dam. Maybe you realized that there's still more.

In fact, it is different for everyone. The important thing now is to feel good about starting the journey. You're beginning to discover who you are and this is what needs to happen in order that you start to ascend to your throne.

As the days go on, I want you to continually reflect on this question. Reflect on your answers to it.

You'll be setting yourself up for an abundance of clarity in all aspects of your life if you do so. Please know, as well, that the answer to this question changes as our lives go on. Yesterday, I was a student struggling to impress her friends and teachers (plus all that that entailed). Today, I am a mother trying to embrace the identity of mentor and teacher. Tomorrow, I can anticipate more changes, but this doesn't scare me or make me think that I'll have to begin the metamorphosis anew because I know that there are aspects of my character that will, (or should), remain consistent. I know that by simply asking the question and tuning in to the answer, I can be flexible to the roles that I find myself in. This, in turn, makes me more able to maximize the pleasure from them so that I can consistently move towards personal growth.

Maybe you've written a biography of yourself before, for a class assignment or personal blog or a job application. This is the same idea, but this is one you'd write for yourself, the human that knows you most personally. There is no need for pretenses, no need to shy away from something, and no need to feel like you'll be judged by your answer.

Who am I?

2

The queen's

modus operandi

*T*here's a sister I know who, at a fairly young age, took on the task of committing the entire Quran to memory. A monumental undertaking for anyone with such a worthy life goal, this young woman was able to do it in less than one year. She was driven to succeed in ways that would astound even the seasoned Quran teacher. And people look at her accomplishment and naturally the number one question they ask is how she did it. Her answer is similar to that of someone who's lost an incredible amount of weight. When asked how they did it, it boils down to less food, more exercise. Less wasted time, more Quran memorization.

Of course, the discipline to stick to a regimented routine is what actually does the trick. So, a better question to ask is *how did you find the discipline to stick to it?* The answer to that question will invariably lead to the question:

What Motivates Me?

Finding the answer to this crucial point is equivalent to finding the key that will unlock the secret garden of your most driven self. Finding your primary motivators will give you the knowledge to know what you want and what needs to happen in order for you to get it. To this end, a look at the hierarchy of human needs is in order. Abraham Maslow is the American psychologist most credited with the model and present day authorities in the field simplify it like so:

1. Certainty/Comfort: People need to feel safe and secure and this is the need for certainty coming into play. We need to know that we will have a roof over our heads each night, clean water to bathe in, a pot of coffee brewing at the start of tomorrow morning (okay, that one's mine).

2. Variety: At the same time we want certainty, we also desire variety. There is a paradox here, but the cliché "variety is the spice of life" does have its merits and has earned its esteem as a rule of life. People need excitement in their lives. Day in and day out, same old, same old, can really wear one down and make for a very unsatisfying, boring existence, and in some this can mean death. Can you see the clash with variety and certainty?

3. Significance: People need to feel that they are important to others, that they are recognized, appreciated, and respected. We'll talk more about this in an upcoming chapter, but let me just say here, that there really is no need to cringe on this one. The need for, and drive towards, significance can be an effective catalyst for good. All the girls who were put down in school by someone and who later went on to be class valedictorian might know what I'm talking about.

4. Connection/Love: We are social beings. We need to love and be loved. We need to bond and experience connection with family and friends. Allah declares: "O mankind! We have created you from a male and a female, and made you into nations and tribes, that you may know one another." (Quran 49: 13)

5. Growth: To become better, to improve our skills, to stretch and expand our horizons is to spread our wings. And growing is essential to a life worth living. Perhaps you've known someone who, at retirement, has hit a roadblock and fallen into a sort of depression. Compare that person with seniors who take up a new hobby or register in a community college class. The latter has a

better chance of thriving because he/she is still growing. Continuing to grow means that you aren't beginning to die (figuratively speaking of course).

6. Contribution: The desire to contribute something of worth—to help others or to make the world a better place is a need that humans possess. It manifests itself in the young woman who studies medicine so that she can help women living in extreme poverty in the poorer areas of the world, or the mother who surrenders her son to a lifetime of studying Islam so that he can enlighten the masses. Contribution comes in many forms, and so long as we feel that we are able to contribute, so long as we gain satisfaction from the belief that we are easing the burden of others.

These human needs all serve a purpose in who we are and the quality of how we live our lives. Our very survival depends on having these needs met. Notwithstanding this fact, if you were to truly analyze who you are, you'd find that one (or two) of these needs is more dominant in you. And knowing which one drives you the most can greatly shape who you become, and is necessary to achievement as the queen of Sheba.

Consider Sana and her dinner. If Sana's primary motivation, her dominant need, was certainty, she would cook dinner because at 6 pm every night, she expects a meal on the table. If there was no meal at 6 pm, Sana might not be a happy queen of Sheba. So, she sticks to her routine schedule and is sure to cook dinner every night.

If Sana was the type of person that is easily bored by the humdrum and her dominant need was the one for variety, what might she do? Sana could check out the new Thai restaurant, or try a recipe she pulled off the internet five minutes ago because it looked interesting. Or perhaps Sana has no time to eat. She's going bungee jumping for the first time tonight.

If Sana's was big on the significance aspect, she could

have her dinner being judged for a blue ribbon ceremony on the local food station. Or maybe she just wants her dad to think she's a better cook than her mom. *"Isn't that the best macaroni and cheese you've ever had?"* When her father agrees, Sana is content. Yummy! It is amazingly delicious, and even her mom jumps on the bandwagon, thinking aloud: *"Maybe we should enter this in a blue ribbon ceremony on the local food station?"* Sana is jumping for joy. She wants to cook dinner every night.

If Sana was big on love and connection, she might gather all her friends and go for pizza, or a picnic in the park. For her, it's not about the meal, so much as what the meal brings in way of bringing the people she cares about together.

And as she gets older, Sana might realize the need for growth and it may become more of a deciding factor. Her dinner might be one she makes during a class with an expert chef who teaches the art of French cooking, so different from the Indian cuisine she's known for so long.

Finally, if Sana reached a point in her life where contribution was paramount, she might spend her dinner at a homeless shelter, giving out food for the hungry.

Like Sana's need for dinner manifesting itself in different, but equally successful ways, the knowledge of who you are and what your primary motivation is can be used by you to achieve all your goals. The awareness of it is fantastic and can flow over into major decisions in your life. Knowing your dominate motivators can help you choose a course of study and a career. They can help you get clarity on what you want for the relationships you have or will have. From the mundane to the major, driving your ambitions and emotions through the filter of your most influential motivator can positively impact all areas of your life. It's a natural add on to the questions you've been pondering from the last chapter and it will allow you to harness the information to your advantage.

Consider Maryam, a woman greatly moved by love and connection. She didn't know this before she chose to take on an office job that has her working from 9 to 5 in a secluded cubicle. She feels stuck now because she does need the money and has decided that there is no way she can quit. When she lets on that she has a deadline coming up for a project that she's been putting off because it will have her working at home after hours, I ask her to use the knowledge of her primary motivators to turn around her perspective. Instead of: *this project is so dreadful, it will take from my time with my family,* she will say: *I am going to finish this project by Friday and the money I earn from it will allow me to take my family for a vacation where all of us will really benefit from the quality time together.* Maryam was more inclined to get it done quickly and the extra money was something she was able to put towards something more valuable to her.

Then there's Noora, who was finding it difficult to connect with her new husband. The long nights he spent hanging out with his buddies was a source of hurt and fast becoming a problem. Why, she wondered, wasn't he able to show his love for her? She'd make him blue ribbon meals and get nary a compliment. She'd just completed her university degree and was shocked that he didn't want to place an announcement of it in the local newspaper. When Noora was able to step back and realize (as you likely already have) that her greatest motivator was significance and his was love and connection, she was able to devise activities that would measure high for the both of them. In lieu of the announcement, Noora began to plan a party. It was a great meeting point for their primary motivators because she would be receiving kudos from so many and he would be grateful that all his family and friends were together for such a fest.

The inevitable question always arises: what motivating need is best? Which one would give me the greatest potential out of life and ensure that I will always be a high achiever and release my inner queen of Sheba? My answer would be that anyone can win the race. It's not as if one is superior to the other, it's that recognizing which is most descriptive of you will give you that head start when you need it. It's about having a strategy and knowing when and how it will work for you.

Protocol 2

Answer these questions in your journal:

To relax, I like to...
I'm most happy when I...
When on the internet, I...
The things that make me angry or upset are...
I feel proud when...
My greatest accomplishment to this date is:
If I had to pinpoint one factor about my personality that drove me to this accomplishment it would be:
This is why I believe that this was the factor:

How did that go? Were you able to decipher what your dominant personality need is? Some of the questions above were meant to get you to start thinking about the applicable, everyday manifestations of this need.

So, for example, if you said that while online you spend much of your time interacting with friends (perhaps on a social networking site, or through the chatting feature) that would be a clear indication that you seek love and connection. Someone might say: I have to spend less time on the internet, and keep saying that and then wonder why she is unable to pull herself away from the computer screen. If she's big on love and connection, and feeling disconnected from friends and family because she's away for school, and students around her are busy writing essays or studying for exams, it won't be easy to give up her computer time. However, if she was able to find another outlet that would fulfill this need, maybe a study group on campus, where like-minded girls get together, she's more likely to minimize the time she wastes chatting online – and still fulfill her dominant personality need. Again, it's about recognizing the practical applications and utilizing them to your advantage.

The other questions are meant to evoke the emotional attachment you have when it comes to your primary needs being met. What feelings, whether negative or positive, come into play when you start analyzing the situations and scenarios of your life?

The last three questions are meant to have you see that when it comes to tangible results, there was a certain drive in place. What was it?

As you begin to decipher the code (hopefully an easy task), you begin to map out a play for your success.

3

Silence!

The queen is thinking!

*L*earning to question any negative thoughts that hold you back from having the inner fortitude to release your inner queen of Sheba is paramount to your success. By negative thoughts, I'm talking about the ones that cause tightness in your chest, a feeling of helplessness, or the ones that drive you to the freezer for a pint (or two) of ice cream in the wee hours of the morning.

Thoughts like:
'I hate my (fill in the blank)'
'I'm worried about (fill in the blank)'
'I won't be able to accomplish (fill in the blank)'
'I'm horrible for thinking/doing/saying (fill in the blank)'
'Nobody cares about me'

Now, forget the thoughts and consider these facts:
Humans prefer stories to statistics.
We seek to confirm, rather than question our ideas.
We oversimplify our thinking.
We often misconstrue events happening around us.

We underestimate the role of outside factors when looking at the results of specific objectives. The first time I presented a live *'Release Your Inner Queen of Sheba'* event, I started with a phrase that most have heard only in its derogatory form.
"Who does she think she is, the queen of Sheba?"
Can't you just see her? She walks in the room, and there's something about her that exemplifies the word

'presence.' She's not the most beautiful woman in the room. Cinderella, over on the other side, serving hors d'oeuvres, is much more so. She's not the smartest woman either. Dalia wrote her thesis on electromagnetic field simulation of trans-cranial magnet stimulation. She's not the best dressed, or the richest. Our heroine, she who thinks she's the queen of Sheba, is not the funniest, or even the most unpleasant.

What she has is presence. She has something that those looking at her (and sarcastically making snide comments about her thinking that she's 'all that') wished they had.

She thinks she's the queen of Sheba.
And if you're to believe the concept of 'I think, therefore I am,' is she then not the Queen of Sheba? She thinks she's a queen of Sheba, and so, in essence, she is a queen of Sheba.

Everything is in your thoughts, in your mind. Your thoughts form who you are. If those thoughts are positive ones, then you are a positive person. If those thoughts dictate negativity towards yourself, then you are that fat, ugly, dumb, so-NOT-a-queen-of-Sheba-and-I'm-depressed-about-it woman that you believe yourself to be. But somehow, I know that that isn't what you want. I know it, because you're reading these words right now. You want to be that competent queen of Sheba with a presence that is so marvelous, beauty queens like Cinderella and professors like Dalia wish they had it.

Yet, believe that if you are a Cinderella or a Dalia, whether you are a beauty queen or a professor, or a mother, or a wife, or a business woman, (or all of the above), if you think you can be a queen of Sheba, then so can you be. This is an important message, because, believe it or not, there are women so beautiful, who, in their heads, live in a world of ugliness. There are ridiculously rich women, who, in their heads, are a few dollars away from total 'beggar in the street' status.

"The mind can make a heaven out of hell or a hell out of heaven." – John Milton

Consider then an average woman who lives at the mercy of the commonplace routine of everyday life. She, who, in her head, is the happiest woman when her toddler kisses her cheek after she's cleaned up yet another of his cups of spilled milk. She, who, in her head, feels so beautiful, if she can only fit in a ten minute shower - and brush her teeth. She, who, in her head, thinks she's smart, because she's just read the latest issue of a health magazine, and knows to add spinach to her shopping cart because the flavonoids will help protect her against age-related memory loss. She, who, because it gives her joy, often quotes this authentic hadith, the words of her Lord through the Prophet Muhammad, peace be upon him:

Allah Almighty has said: "I am as My servant thinks I am. I am with him when he makes mention of Me. If he makes mention of Me to himself, I make mention of him to Myself; and if he makes mention of Me in an assembly, I make mention of him in an assembly better than it. And if he draws near to Me an arm's length, I draw near to him a fathom's length. And if he comes to Me walking, I go to him at speed."

"I am as My servant thinks I am." If even the idea of the role our Creator plays in our lives is directly related to how we perceive Him to be, then what then of how you think you are?

There's this whole idea and culture built upon the catchphrase "think positive!" And that's fine for those who are inclined to do so, but for those who struggle with thoughts of the negative variety, it can be such a drag to hear that one over and over again. They're thinking "I'm ugly, nobody loves me," and "there's no hope for me, my life is a failure," and you want to say "think positive"? It's like asking a child to figure out how E=mc2. Likewise, "think positive" is meaningless when one is embroiled in such paralyzing thoughts. A better statement would be:

"Don't believe everything you think!"

When we learn to question our negative thoughts, we learn to loosen the grip they have on us. Evidence shows that negative thoughts never did lead to the release of any queen of Sheba, or much else for that matter. What "I'm so hideous, if he were to look at me he'd puke," thought led to a girl winning the hand of a handsome suitor? What "I'm so stupid, there's no way I'll ever figure out algebra," thought lead to an advanced degree in mathematics? What "I will always fail no matter whatever diet I try," thought lead to a successful weight loss strategy?

When I say "don't believe everything you think," I'm not referring to the things that you say to yourself that are designed to incite/scare/challenge you into taking action, if only to disprove them (ex. a *'I'm such a flat slob, I'll fail at every diet'* thought meant to kick start your latest diet Monday). By the way, even if taking the desired action is the end result, this method isn't recommended to begin with – usually because results are short term. Your heart is smarter than your mind thinks it is. I'm talking about the thoughts that truly hold you back from being the best you can be.

Perhaps you can recall a time when you were so misguided in a thought you had, and when you realized the truth about it, you smacked yourself on the head for what you previously had believed to be the truth. Maybe it was "oh, I'm such a drag to be around, my husband hates spending time with me," when in reality, he was out buying you a special gift. Oftentimes, we make such presumptions with others and when we realize the truth, we forget about it, and it doesn't affect our relationships in the long run. Isn't it about time we gave ourselves that same benefit of the doubt?

Protocol 3

Take out your journal. By now, it should fondly be known as "your best friend."

1. Write down any negative thought you harbor.
2. Ask yourself, 'is it absolutely, completely 100% true?' How do you know? Can you think of times when it wasn't?
3. What do you do when you believe that thought? What happens? How do you treat others? How do you treat yourself when you believe that thought?

***As you ponder over the answers, close your eyes and really allow yourself to feel the pain of this thought. See yourself carrying the thought with you for a long time. ***

__Now, stop writing and do a plié, ballerina style.__

Come back to this now. What's up with the ballet move, you wonder? The idea is to get you to realize that breaking the hold on a negative thought is possible. And if you weren't distracted enough with that, consider (and answer) the following:

4. Who would you be without that thought? How would you be different if you didn't believe that thought?
5. Now turn the thought around. Do a complete 'polar opposite' thought switch up. Ex. "I'm ugly" becomes "I'm beautiful."

***Really allow yourself to feel the joy and levity of the new thought. See yourself carrying the thought with you for a long time. ***

6. Ask yourself: How wonderful of a queen of Sheba will you be with this thought?

7. Think of examples of how this thought is true.

8. Now, commit to believing this thought because it is the truer one and the one that will best serve you.

You can follow the same process for any and all negative thoughts you have. It works best when you're completely conscious of the pain and harm a thought can cause and how when you turn it around, you set yourself free, and encourage positivity that will allow you to flourish. You're unshackling your mind and your potential when you do so.

4

The queen's

eye view

Wondrous are the believer's affairs. For him there is good in all his affairs, and this is so only for the believer. When something pleasing happens to him, he is grateful, and that is good for him; and when something displeasing happens to him, he is patient, and that is good for him."
- The Prophet Muhammad, peace be upon him

When I was 18 years old and pregnant, my husband packed all our possessions in the car and we headed east to start our life. Everything we owned was in that car; there was a stereo, 2 suitcases filled with clothes, a couple of pillows, a brand new dish set, and a box of junk food. We had a couple of hundred dollars in our pockets, and exactly $33 left in our bank account. We were planning to drive for 12 hours, stop at a hotel room overnight and then continue on until we reached our destination. Eleven hours into the trip, and our car broke down. And after spending quite a large chunk of our money to tow it to the nearest town, the mechanic said that it would cost thousands to fix.

U-Frame-It was an art décor franchise that was quite popular back in the day. Basically, the premise is that you take in your art, choose your frame, install it yourself, and out you go. Of course, you pay a price, but the effect your frame will have on your artwork is entirely up to you. How does this concern you? In our lives, bad (seemingly out of our control) things happen, and it is not so much as how or why they happen, but it is how we contextualize, or frame them that make a difference in how they affect us.

Now that I've studied the methodology of success

principles, I know that there are tools and resources we can learn in order to help ourselves and others to reframe situations and events so that (like the last protocol) a new frame is put around harmful ones. Still, these tools and resources were not at my disposal when we were stranded on that highway road, (just don't ask me how long ago that was). But there was a certain verse in the Quran that I kept on repeating back then, in the thick of the crisis, a verse I've oft repeated since:

"...And it is possible that you dislike a thing which is good for you, and that you love a thing which is bad for you. But Allah knows, and you know not." (Quran 2:216)

I kept thinking, *thank God, things could have been much worse.* Cars can be replaced. Money comes and goes.

Till this very day, I look back on that situation and I remember how my husband walked miles to get me a decent meal and spent much of what he had left on it. I remember feeling grateful that the stereo survived. I remember feeling the spirit of human kindness from those who empathized along the way to our destination. I found strength that day, and know that I can have control over the frames in my life.

Reframing is a skill that all queens of Sheba should have. In its simplest form, reframing is the ability to find ways to see a problem from a different perspective. It is how you change a negative into a positive.

To illustrate, consider Abdullah, who was hit by a car, causing him injuries that would confine him to his bed for the six months. Now, it would seem like this a major negative, correct? But the reality was that Abdullah was having marital trouble. His wife felt like he wasn't around for her and their young son. He loved them and wanted to be with them, but he was working 2 jobs to pay off a debt he had incurred while in school. Worst of all, he complained of a lack of feeling connected spiritually, and was feeling the faithfulness he'd previously taken for granted was suffering.

If you were to meet Abdullah today, he'd happily declare that being hit by that car was the best thing that ever happened to him. How, you're wondering? Being bed ridden for that length of time forced him to spend quality time with his family and their relationship blossomed. His financial situation improved because of the settlement money from the car driver. And best of all, his close encounter with death really made him see how he needed to reconnect with his faith and spirituality. Abdullah's story is an extreme one, but you can apply the same principles to anything that needs to be looked at in a new light, any situation that needs a new frame.

During live 'release your inner queen of Sheba' events, I give out seemingly difficult situations and then ask participants to think of positive spins on them. A doctor's diagnosis indicating that someone has 6 months to live becomes a blessing, an advanced warning so that that person can take care of the things needed to be taken care of before death. A husband walking out on his family could be an opportunity for the children to be spared a lifetime of abuse his presence would have caused. A job lay-off could turn into a chance to explore a dormant talent with more money earning potential than ever.

It's all about the frames you put around situations. And when you're able to put a pretty one around them, even the ugliest pictures can shine, or at least become tolerable to look at. At its very best, the art of reframing can be used not only to get over negative situations, but also to harness your strength so that you can use them to your advantage. You can surprise your most negative self with the things you can do afterwards! Those prettier frames can help you release your inner queen of Sheba sooner than you think!

What meaning do you attach to events or situations?

That is the question.

Amal is a woman with a real fear of public speaking. Once when she was younger, she'd had to do a presentation for her class. At all the wrong points during it, the class had laughed. From the situation, she came out with the idea that if she had to speak in public, she'd be laughed off of the stage. She figured that she was so bad at it, any attempts would simply be a grossly absurd exercise in cruel and unusual self-torture. But this fear, she admitted wearily, had held her back from many a project she was passionate about.

"In fact," she lamented, "all my dreams are being put on the back burner because of my fear of public speaking."

I could hear Amal talking. She was an articulate woman with proficient speaking skills, who, I was certain, could pull off a presentation. *If* she could get over her belief that she'd fail at it. Knowing that she could speak, but fearing that she would fall on her face, Amal was ready to see what could be done and how to undo the damage done in a classroom years before.

To put Amal in a 'reframing' mood, I suggested she focus on answering these questions:

What other explanations can there be for a group of kids laughing during your speech? If your daughter went through the exact same scenario and came home crying, what would you say to her? In what ways can this past situation make you a better speaker now?

Once she began to believe that perhaps the little brats (sorry about that) were possibly engulfed by some silly thing the class clown was doing in the back row (unbeknownst to her) or that maybe someone had given them too much candy, Amal was able to focus on building her public speaking skills. Her starting point was fresher - she didn't have this debilitating picture of people laughing at her in her mind, and she could take it from there. She picked up books on the subject and enrolled in a local workshop. Amal scheduled her first practice run with a group of friends at her home, and when they raved about it, she was further able to reinforce that she did indeed have the makings of an articulate presenter.

So it is that the purpose of reframing an event or situation that is making you feel less empowered or even downright destitute, is not to *pretend* that everything is wonderful, rather, the purpose of reframing is to actively get you to come up with strategies or viable solutions to the 'seemingly' negative event or situation.

Protocol 4

It's art time! This is the part when you get really creative.

But before you actually pull out your paints and papers (I do recommend paints for this- but feel free to use your preferred coloring tools), close your eyes and visualize what any negative event or situation would look like. The negative event or situation that needs to undergo a 'reframe' should be one that has disappointed you or held you back in the past.

If you're having trouble envisioning a situation, that's great! Why don't you use an event or situation that has harmed a friend or family member? If you can practice this protocol, you can have a usable skill for life.

Now start putting that vision to paper. You can do so without having any art skills (just ask me), so, for example, if someone got a frightening medical diagnosis, a painting of the word 'cancer' with blood dripping down would be a start.

After you've completed paining the situation/event, put a twist on it. The changes you make are completely up to you. It's your work of art. But for demonstration purposes, here are some ideas:

1. Make it larger or smaller than what you saw in your mind's eye;
2. Change the colors around; perhaps what should have been red becomes green;
3. Add a funny character to the picture; does anyone remember Woody the Woodpecker? Who can you add?
4. Make the border something decorative, e.g. continuous happy faces or flowers galore

When your masterpiece is complete, reflect on these two key questions:

1. *How has the actual visual that you can touch altered the visual in your mind?*
2. *As the queen of Sheba, how would you describe what you learned from this exercise?*

5

Beauty Queen

5

Beauty Queen

$\mathscr{J}$f the number one thing men want more of is money, then for women, it's probably better looks. Maybe those are sweeping generalizations, but maybe they are not. The negative views women have about their looks have been documented in study after study, and one recent one that polled over 6000 women in 21 different countries concluded that a mere 2% would describe themselves as physically attractive. The results are to the delight of (among others) the cosmetics industry, the diet industry, and the plastic surgery industry as well. Even countries that are predominately Muslim have alarming rates of women going under the knife in an attempt to measure up to some 'ideal'.

Who created this ideal? The purpose of this book is not to disperse blame or muddle too much in the root causes of a problem, but rather to stoke solutions. Still, it's an 'ideal' that we should be rebelling against, especially as it is imposed upon us unfairly and causes us, as individuals, to want to change the way we were created. And it's definitely not conducive to releasing your inner queen of Sheba when you feel like you're ugly by societal 'norms.'

"Beauty is in the eye of the beholder," is a belief I've held for as long as I can remember, and it's still a good one. When women are conditioned to compare themselves to an arbitrary standard, we all lose. Beauty does come in all colors, in all shapes, and in countless faces. And it is for the smart eye of the beholder, the beautiful eye of the beholder, who can recognize the beauty in others, to behold it.

Now, if only we could be that beholder, and recognize

the beauty in ourselves. Alas, this may in fact be much
more difficult than it sounds. Recently, for a special outing,
my three-year-old daughter put on a new dress, some new
barrettes in her hair, and a spray of lovely perfume. In what
can only be described as an instinctive act (at least I don't
think I've ever done it so she can't have been mimicking
me), she ran to her father, twirled and asked, "how do I
look?" Daddy was quick with the compliments that pleased
her. Still, it wasn't enough. She then proceeded to her
older brother and asked him the same question. "How do I
look?" Unfortunately, my son hadn't yet been trained on the
appropriate male response, and when he failed to say that
she was "the most beautiful three-year-old girl in a pink
flowered dress and silver barrettes in her hair" that he had
ever seen, she broke down. She cried and cried. Her
reaction taught my son how to answer and I'm sure in the
future when a woman asks him how she looks, he'll
think twice and take her sensitivity into consideration.

Why do we do this to ourselves? The incident
underscored the fact that not only do women have an inner
desire to look beautiful, but we also seem to have an inborn
sense that loveliness is a virtue that we must work hard to
achieve (even as three-year-olds). It also points to the fact
that the female variety is acutely susceptible to the opinions
of others when it comes to accepting ourselves as beautiful.
When you interact with women as a daily requirement of
your job and preach that self-perception is so utterly
important, it becomes such an uphill battle trying to
convince them that they can be the beholder of their own
beauty.

I actually spent much time and effort debating on
whether or not to even include this chapter in the book,
especially when it came to having it take precedence (in
chronological order that is) over the next chapter, which I
believe is even more crucial to releasing your inner queen of
Sheba. But time and again, I'm faced with how women's

perception of their looks holds them back – it's almost criminal how much so.

In a world that is arguably increasingly turning to the vain and shallow, women who feel they are downright 'ugly' set themselves up for failure in every sense of the word. And sadly, 'I'm ugly' is the ugly (pun not intended) reality that is found when so many of us look really deep for the truth behind what holds us back from living our best life, pursuing our goals, and becoming that queen of Sheba.

It's a misperception that will ultimately lead to ruin.

The train of thought might sound something like this: "I'm ugly, so I'm unlovable... And if I'm unlovable, I'll be alone... If being alone is the result of my life, how does anything I do matter?" Ironically, believing we are ugly can actually ensure that we will be alone, that our accomplishments will indeed be unacceptable, and that happiness will always evade us.

So, if you find yourself falling into this trap, it's time to find a way to change your mind. You have to dig your way back to believing that you are beautiful. And I don't care if you look like the wicked witch who offered Snow White the poisoned apple, you are beautiful. If you believe that Allah created you in 'the best of forms', how can you not be?

Often, someone will admit to believing they're ugly, but when you see them face to face, you'll wonder if they are seeing the same thing you're seeing when they look into their mirror. If beauty is in the eye of the beholder, what do you see when you look into *your* mirror?

Protocol 5

This one is as simple as looking into a mirror. You can do it in the morning after you've brushed your teeth and washed your face. Or in the evening when you've just had a nice soak after an especially productive day in which you've begun to release your inner queen of Sheba. The time doesn't matter, what does is that you're mentally ready for this simple, but profound exercise.

As you study your reflection, you think of 3 to 5 things that make you beautiful. You do this every day for the next 3 weeks, each time thinking of new things. Maybe it's your killer smile, or the arc of your feet. Perhaps it's the almond shape of your jet black eyes or the length of your graceful neck. Or the money you put aside each month to sponsor an orphan a world away. I don't know, you know. Behold it. See the beauty reflected in that mirror. And thank your Lord for creating you in the best of forms.

If it's hard to do at first, persist. If it's easy at first, but then gets hard, persist. If it seems ridiculous, call me ridiculous, laugh at me, but still persist. I want this to be a breeze for you, so keep on persisting. The point is that you push yourself to make new connections, establish new beliefs about your beauty.

If it's hard to do this in front of the mirror, then take out your journal and reflect on the following: *times that people complimented the way you look even if you didn't believe them; times that you felt beautiful- what was going on then? What needs to happen now in order to regain that feeling?*

Now take your ideas to the mirror. And do it again and again. For twenty-one days, build on that habit of beholding your own beauty. The end game is that you win the pageant and you won't need validation from that mirror anymore. You will know that you look good.

6

The woman
who would be queen

'*A*rrogance' is a word with a bad reputation and so many negative connotations. Sadly, the word 'confidence' comes too close to it for most women to recognize the difference. The fear of being seen as arrogant and conceited has stopped many women from achieving to their highest potential. Think of the studious student who pretends not to know the answers to the questions the teacher asks so that she won't be considered a 'know-it-all' and lose friends? You know her, right?

Or how about Camilla, who looks lovely in her new clothes but her mother refuses to compliment her thinking it'll go to her head. *"That is a nice dress"*. Samia lands a plum job that hundreds were vying for. *"It was nothing. I got lucky," she thinks.* Rifqa spends her time trying to feed her hunger for doing good things. *"Oh Allah! I'll never be a good Muslim," she complains.*

Oftentimes, we can't even celebrate the good things in our life because of an almost irrational fear of arrogance.

For Muslim women, the struggle can be even more pronounced because we're instilled with the idea that humbleness is a great virtue. Indeed, humility is a merit; however, the definition of humility in relation to that of arrogance needs a more in-depth analysis. Or a simpler one.

Consider the saying of the Prophet Muhammad, may the peace and blessings of Allah be upon him when asked about the topic:

"Arrogance," he said, "is to reject the truth and to look down on people." (reported by Muslim)

Furthermore, when you look into the lives of some of his companions (including the female ones), you realize that most weren't plagued with the inability to believe in their skills and talents. Take someone like Omar, may Allah be pleased with him. Books have been written about his boldness and strength of character and conviction. He was notorious for being "al farooq," a distinguisher between right and wrong, making a huge impact on the spread of Islam. Omar was an assertive man who consistently knew and expressed his competencies and directives. Indeed, the women in his life had to have had self-confidence to exist and thrive in his domain. Consider his sister Fatima, who became Muslim before he did and refused to let him touch the words of Allah. Consider Hafsa, Omar's daughter, who, when prompted by her father, would admit to upsetting her husband, the prophet. His fury with her was calmed only by the intercession of the Prophet Muhammad (peace be upon him) himself. And then there was Umm Salamah, another female relative who reprimanded Omar, saying "You have interfered in everything. Will you now interfere between the Messenger of Allah and his wives?" Omar, in describing the incident, says that Umm Salamah, "...kept after me until she made me give up much of what I thought proper." (Ibn Kathir)

They were amongst the best of nations and none of these noble companions were known to be arrogant. Confident, capable, commanding, yes. Arrogant, no. So, please, banish the belief that self-confidence and piety can't go hand in hand. All banished? Now, you're free to become that self-assured queen of Sheba you were meant to be.

Admittedly, it may be harder than it sounds, and in fact, in all my reading and research about building your self confidence, no one method or theory proves to be completely and distinctly greater than all the others. Social scientists and experts on the subject will give you a host of techniques, but who is to say what works best for each individual?

Confidence is such a complex trait that trying to box it up in a 'one-size-fits- all' package ridicules the fact that all of us (unless we're newborns) are a culmination of a life time of various experiences and as innumerable as those experiences are, even more so are our reactions to them and the influence they've wielded in our lives. Nevertheless, humans seek to simplify. And so to, does an aspiring queen of Sheba. If a lack of confidence is holding her back for being the best she can be, it must be addressed. It must find its way into this book of protocols. And hopefully, I've designed one that will not only take into consideration a few of the different theories on the matter, but also one that is a natural follow up to the last protocol (remember the mirror one).

If you believe that confidence can be built, then affirmations are one way to do it. Affirmations that take into consideration what kind of learner you are can be especially helpful. So, if you lean to the visual, having a picture of you at your best and constantly looking at it will build confidence. If you are more auditory, repeating positive statements about yourself aloud or hearing others do so, would enhance your confidence.

If confidence is built through achievement, then strategizing ways in which you can gain this most important side benefit has to become a top priority, ensuring that your goals are set up with a realistic plan for making them happen. For example, how would Faiza feel if she was finally able to lose the extra thirty pounds that have been bothering her since the birth of her baby? A boost to her confidence is natural. But what if she made it a near impossible goal to lose that weight by the time her baby is 6 weeks old, and considering all the new mom duties et al., she would be setting herself up for failure and a blow to her self esteem if she fell short of her goal.

Finally, one theory states that the way to gain confidence

is by losing fear. There are a few ways to lose fears, but the best, as the famous quote by Mark Twain so blatantly expresses, is to *"do the thing you fear most and the death of fear is certain."* I won't make you do the thing you fear the most, but I am going to make you undertake an exciting protocol. Check it out.

Protocol 6

The previous protocol should have already begun to set you up for this one. Are you ready? Excellent! This will actually be divided into two parts. For the first part, you'll need that journal. For the second, you'll need some major guts. First, in your journal, please compile the following two lists.

List 1 - These are the things I am good at:
List 2 - These are the things I could work on (also known as not good at - but let's try and stay away from the negative):

As you compile each, really take the time to recall events or situations that prove what you're putting on paper. So, Anisa might write "I'm good at respecting older people." She realizes that this characteristic is a good one because there was the time she got up from her seat on the subway for an old man with a cane. He was so thankful because he'd previously been ignored by everyone else with a seat. Recognizing her head scarf as a mark of her faith, the older gentleman loudly proclaimed,
    "You Muslims are raised proper!"
    Anisa was over the moon because it was a good message for everyone who heard it and it was a direct result of her being good at respecting older people.
    After you've compiled your lists, you'll probably see that

list #1 is much, much longer. This fact should probably already have boosted your confidence. And if it isn't longer, then please feel free to cheat a little. Just kidding! This should be an honest assessment of things you are good at and things you could work on. However, when you take into consideration the protocol for chapter 3 (see how it it's all fitting together), then am I just kidding? The first list should indeed be longer.

Now take a look at the next list. If you could kindly find the one that is easiest to fix and get good at, that would be great. That's the one we're working with for part 2 of this protocol.

You're going to take that one thing and come up with one challenge. The challenge should take you out of your journal, and preferably into an open space. The challenge must adhere to the following criteria:

- it must involve another person
- it must take you out of your comfort zone (but stay within stay within good girl boundaries)

You have to use your creativity here. The next step is to go out and just do it! As you're going out and doing it, continually affirm to yourself that you're doing it. Continually affirm to yourself that Allah wants you to be the best that you can be. Continually affirm that HE has given you the will, and the brain, and the gift of confidence to do what you set out to do. Continually tell yourself that you are the queen of Sheba, capable and confident. And do the challenge.

Anisa's challenge involved applying for a job at her local library. She didn't have any of the proper credentials either. Anisa's parents paid for all her expenses, so it wasn't about needing the job. She just felt like having one would help her build independence in all areas of her life (certainly a confidence enhancer). Plus, she's a true book lover; even as a child she would day-dream about being locked all night in a library. For her, getting this job would rank high on the achievement meter.

To make her challenge fulfill the criteria, Anisa took her resume and didn't just submit it for consideration. She spoke to the head administrator there and asked that she be given a chance to prove herself despite not having the correct requirements. Anisa even shared her childhood fantasy.

You're curious as to whether or not she got the job, but that isn't the point, but rather that she had done something she never would have acted on before, and that she felt stronger and more confident in the process.

Now, what's YOUR challenge?

If you're feeling stumped, perhaps Anisa can recommend a good book to inspire you.

7

Coronation

*S*hadia really laments the past, tries not to think about it, and in fact, refuses to talk about the details. But they emerge, little by little, and despite her best intentions to keep them hidden from the world. No one in the community knew her before she became Muslim a few years ago. One day, she showed up in the mosque and asked to take her declaration of faith. And when prompted (as new Muslims often are) to share her "How I found Islam" story, she claimed that she'd always had a desire to "find a connection to her creator." Her heart was opened.

So, one day, I was there with a group of sisters, having what I assumed was a casual conversation, but apparently I'm in "listen to me talk mode" more often than I think I am. Basically, we were talking about the roles that parents play in the lives of their daughters and how the roles that they take on can either make or break an innocent little girl. I said something along the lines of:

"Ideally, the father should allow his daughter to indeed be his little princess. The father should always celebrate her accomplishments, tell her she's beautiful and protect her like she's a rare gem. It sets her up for knowing how her husband should be treating her in the future. And the mother is the one that should be the example for her daughter. She should be that accomplished, beautiful, precious gem who knows how to treat herself."

Lo and behold, Shadia visibly breaks down, and rushes to the ladies room. The other sisters turn to me all accusatory like, as if to say, *look what you've done* - but even they don't understand what has happened. At long last, Shadia emerges and asks to speak to me privately. She wants to share her story.

Apparently, she'd never known her father and her mother was constantly walking the fine line between temporary insanity and dismal drunkenness. It really got me thinking about the stories we perpetrate in our heads and how we allow them to be the 'masters' of our lives. Anyhow, Shadia asked a question that was a sure cry for help.

"Is it possible for me to ever get over this feeling that I'm worthless and feel like that precious, strong woman who had those amazing parents?"

There was a reason I used the word 'ideal' to begin with. Because, despite the fact that there are those who did have the benefit of having wonderful parents who worked hard to make them who they are, there are just as many of us who did not. Without a doubt, it's much easier to claim your crown if you've already inherited it. But that shouldn't take away from she who earns the crown through sheer will and determination. And, I'd be willing to back the fact that the latter queen of Sheba may indeed value her earned role much more than the one who was simply born into it. But in both, there is good.

Abu Hurayra said that the Messenger of Allah, peace be upon him, said: "The strong believer is better and more beloved to Allah than the weak believer, although there is good in each. Desire that which will bring you benefit, and seek help from Allah and do not give way to incapacity. If something happens to you, do not say, 'If only I had done such-and-such.' Rather say, 'The decree of Allah. He does what He will.' Otherwise you will open yourself up to the acts of Shaytan (the devil)." (reported by Muslim)

I'm telling you, despite your story, whether good, bad, or ugly, you can become that precious, strong woman. Forget about your story and live in this moment. From this moment, on. From this moment on, you are the queen of

Sheba. Are you ready to claim your crown? Welcome to your coronation!

Protocol 7

Remember when you were a little girl and you had dreams of becoming a fashion model? You sashayed around your bedroom with your best dress on, and practiced walking straight with a book on your head. No?

Okay, well, you're going to do it now.

Step 1: Find a heavy book that is pretty large in diameter (or is that just for circles? Well, I mean square. The point being that you don't want it to easily fall off your head.)
Step 2: Place it firmly on your head as you stand at one end of your room.
Step 3: Proceed to walk to the other end of the room, taking deliberate steps to ensure that the book doesn't fall off your head.
Step 4: If the book does begin to slip, stop. Close your eyes. Catch it before it tumbles all the way to the ground.
Step 5: Proceed from step 2, and continue on.
Step 6: Do this for 5 minutes.
Step 7: Repeat daily until you can do it with your eyes closed and not drop the book once.

Now, take out your journal and answer this question: "What did I learn from this exercise?" or if you'd prefer, "What is that (-insert wonderful adjective here-) Heba Alshareef trying to teach me?"

What you do or do not learn, or how you benefit from this exercise is so individual and I've heard so many different responses. One sister recently told me that she still does the exercise, months after I formally introduced it to her. She doesn't necessarily place the book on her head, but she does get in perfect form, closes her eyes, and walks back and forth, with deliberate steps. Sometimes, she says, she imagines herself acting with dignity in a stressful work situation. Sometimes, she says, she plays out scenarios of imaginary dates she will have with her husband to be. Even though she isn't yet married or engaged, she sees someone loving her deeply and treating her right. Another sister writes that the exercise is like a break for her, a time to really focus on recharging. It makes her feel like all the stress of housekeeping and childrearing can disappear. For those five minutes, she continues, she isn't a 'frazzled' housewife and mother wearing flannel pajamas and avoiding a sink full of dishes. For those five minutes, she's nobody, and yet, somebody truly special. And when the five minutes is over, it's okay that she's wearing flannel pajamas and she gets to those dishes with a weird sort of energy. Someone else tells me she does it before she goes to the gym, and somehow it puts her in the right mood for a workout.

Regardless of individual benefits, women agree that this is five minutes that they give to themselves. It is five minutes where they can focus on five minutes. They are conscious that these are the moments that are indicative of what can always be.

What I hope to teach by it is that 'from this moment' you are stepping onto the stage at your own crowning. May Allah bless your reign!

Part Two

If life is defined it it's most simplistic form as getting from point A to point B, knowing the location of point B is sure to make arriving much easier. In the previous chapters we dealt with point A, as in beginning to understand where our starting points are. We worked on protocols that would build our confidence levels and banish negative thoughts that would delay the emergence of our inner queen of Sheba. And we spent some time getting to know ourselves and the needs that drive us.

Now, our focus is on taking what we've learned and developing a hard core strategy for what we want our lives to be. You'll be defining your point B and learning precisely how to move towards it.

People ask me what amazes me about the original queen of Sheba so much, and I say that she was one smart woman. Let me explain.

When last we visited the story, the hoopoe bird was sent to the kingdom of Saba to deliver the message from his master, and the queen was about to open it and read, all under the watchful gaze of the carrier. Bilqis opens the letter and to her court she reads aloud, "it is from Solomon, and it is in the name of Allah, most beneficial, most merciful." After the spectacular opening, Solomon goes on to demand her immediate appearance in surrender to his forces and kingdom.

Now, Bilqis, you realize, is responsible for an entire people, a thriving land. Surrender is not what a smart woman does. So, she poses the matter to her advisors, saying, "I have not decided upon a matter except that I take your counsel." She was willing to listen to what they had to say. Those advisors (maybe all male) were ready for war. They declared that if Solomon wanted a fight, they'd give him a fight. They boasted of their strength. But the queen was a smart one. She had the long term in mind when she duly noted that, "kings when they enter a country despoil it and make the noblest of its people the lowest." And in the very same verse from the Quran, Allah, agrees with the queen's statement, saying "and indeed that is what they do." Bilqis, with the end game in mind, decides on a very wise course of action declaring, "I'm going to send him some presents and wait to see with what news return my ambassadors." (Quran 27: 29-35)

Having the ability to see the bigger picture and knowing the where you're headed is having the right mindset that it takes to be present and calm and utilize *the* best strategies that will get you there, at your point B.

You're going to love this part. It's when you roll up your sleeves and get REALLY excited about the process and the possibilities. The sky is blue, the sun is shining, the birds are singing. Right here is your spring, and the way to find your castle. You'll want to dance your way there. Can I come along?

8

Eye on the crown

The sea takes your breath away. As you stand upon its shores, you absorb the silliness of the waves. At times they come in with a fury so strong it slaps your body and you move back thinking that your feet might get wet, but they are already wet. The sand that runs through your toes is wet. Your clothes are wet, even the scarf that covers your hair is moist to the touch. The salty mist envelops you and you suddenly feel very thirsty. And you think that perhaps you should go, you've wasted enough time, just standing there, on the sea's periphery, watching the waves come in. *Just one more,* something inside of you pleads. And you listen to it. And you aren't displeased. This wave comes trickling in slowly. It barely touches your feet before rolling back in. It's teasing you, mocking you, knowing that you haven't had enough, and knowing that you won't be able to pull away just yet, knowing that even the essential need for food or drink won't deter you. *Just one more.*

If you've ever been to a beautiful place in your life that had you thinking, *Glory be to Allah, I wonder what the actual paradise must look like, I want you to go back there now.* I mean literally take your journal and go back there. But if that place is literally thousands of miles away and you can't get there today, then there is no need to fret. Just think of a substitute.

The most beautiful thing about beautiful scenery is that it usually inspires us. It has us connecting so many dots and feeling such harmony. If a husband has just had a big fight with his wife, a walk in the fresh air would likely have him come back home calmer, and more ready to find a solution. If a family wants to spend quality time together, have fun, and make memories that would last for generations, they might go on a camping trip together. A stressed employee might take lunch in the park because the natural surroundings might mean a tranquil break in the day. A student who takes a year off for traveling before beginning university can open up his/her horizons and have the experience help decide what he/she really wants for the future.

This leads me to the meat of this chapter: the vision. It's all about the vision. And if you can clearly define your vision, then you have got it made. I talk much about vision and how it is essential to being, doing, and having all that you want in this life and hopefully in the next as well. Maybe you already have a clear vision. Maybe you've been looking for one. Maybe you can't decide. Maybe you'd like to ask the audience.

At times, people will look into life-coaching or help when they feel like something in their life needs to change. They may feel that they're just going around in circles and all the scenery looks the same, and it isn't of the inspiring variety. They know they need goals, they know they need a point B, they know they need a vision for their lives, but for some reason, they haven't been able to define it. They haven't discovered what would make them love their life and savor everyday simply because they're working towards the realization of that vision. And they're hoping that a coach will tell them what their vision should be.

Sorry to say it, but that's a futile hope. Vision comes from within you. You decide. Others may influence your thoughts about it, perhaps even help you mold it, but, at the end of the day, it is you who has to live it. And if you've decided that it is not a fun one, that it is a futile waste of your time and might cause complete and utter misery, then it's a dumb vision to hold on to because you'll never do anything with it. You'll need to: "Get a life! Get a vision!"

When you finally find your 'right' vision, your life will never be the same. You'll have such purpose and drive, that you may wake up in the mornings much earlier than usual and perhaps even without the aid of an alarm clock.

Sadly (or, expectedly) your vision may change. Parts of it may be forgotten, or replaced entirely by a new one. Other aspects of it may not have been in your destiny, and you may have to let go. Life may not always cooperate with your vision and sometimes you might feel like the vision you've decided upon is just plain stupid or far-fetched. Who knows, maybe it is. But who am I to tell you that? Who is that one person who always likes to bring you down to do that? And who is your own 'negative thought' inner voice to do that either? It's your vision, first and foremost. You get to decide it.

For one sister, her supreme vision had her walking the halls of her very own orphanage. She really felt this was something she wanted to work towards, something that she'd long dreamed of, something that would give her satisfaction in this life and hopefully bring her the mercy of Allah in the next. Another sister's vision included taking her large family and living on a farm with all of them working the land together. She saw herself enjoying grandchildren there, and teaching each of them about Islam so that they'd be able to teach others. But all of them would come together at the end of the day to eat at the large supper table. Yet another sister wanted to win a prestigious award for her contributions in her field of study and research. She was a chemistry student who'd been working on her PhD and considered Marie Curie's two Nobel peace prizes an inspiration. "Imagine if I could be the first Muslim woman to do something like that," she dreamt aloud.

If you can dream it, if you can picture it, if you can visualize it, you're on your way to yours. There's something so liberating about finally connecting to that dream. I can't tell you what that feels like, but I pray that you find it soon. Or maybe you've already found it, but have buried it somewhere beneath responsibilities or life's tasks that consume your time. Or maybe you're frightened of failure, or maybe even success. But if you don't do this, not much else will seem important. You set a vision so that you can start appreciating the scenery. *And the waves upon your feet.*

Protocol 8

Block off a day without distractions. A day might not be enough, but it's a start. Take your journal to that place we talked about at the start of the chapter, the one that inspires you to no end. Smell the fresh air; allow the mercy of Allah to fill you with gratitude for your life. For everything you have and for every blessing known to you that you can think of, thank HIM. Ask yourself the following questions:

Who do I want to be?
What experiences do I want to have on this earth?
What do I want to leave behind after I've gone?

Instinctively, you'll dig deep to find the answers. You'll search dreams you've buried. You'll revisit ideas you've stumbled upon. You'll wonder and wonder, until you find your passion. Once you've answered the questions completely (either today, or next month, or whenever you're ready), I want you to really envision the vision. Close your eyes. Walk into the vision.

See it. Hear it. Touch it. Smell it. Taste it.

Truly savor what the vision means to you and then allow yourself to feel the joy of that vision. Be drawn into it like an infant who can't resist a piece of colorful candy. Be pulled into it like iron being forced into a magnetic field.
Remain in that vision...

9

The queen's a posteriori

$\mathcal{R}$emain in that vision... isn't it sweet? Now flip the switch and turn off the lights! See nothing anymore. The vision is gone. You are fumbling in the dark, trying desperately to find your way, but there is nothing. No sight, no sound, no smell, no taste of it - gone it is, all gone! You feel helpless, like you can't catch your breath, but before you have an anxiety attack, I'd like you to open your eyes and come back to now. You're back in your surroundings, your journal still in hand. Your vision is a distant memory. Your task is done. You can go home now. Thank-you.

Are you feeling content with that? Or are you really mad at me right now? If you're feeling content with turning the light off on that vision, then I'm afraid, you have to go back and redo the last protocol, because you haven't gotten the right vision.

If you feel like you could punch me in the nose, well that's not very nice. But I understand and I will not hold it against you. Congratulations! I think you have unearthed your vision. Now it's a matter of realizing why it's so important that you achieve it. The purpose, or the a posteriori, behind it is what will drive you towards making it happen. If your purpose isn't strong enough, then you're not likely to do the work needed to achieve the desired result.

When Hannan saw that her dear friend Ronda was losing an exuberant amount of weight on the latest diet craze, she wanted to do it to. Hannan figured that if she could lose a quick 10 pounds, she'd feel really good - especially if she could enjoy that chocolate cheesecake at her favorite deli without any guilt. So, Hannan got the essentials from Ronda. She even went out and bought the necessary diet staples and when Ronda suggested they go the buddy route and do their weigh-ins together, Hannan was really excited. Ronda had said that she'd lost 10 pounds in her first week on the diet.

Sadly, one week later, Ronda had lost 2 pounds and Hannan had lost only 1. What went wrong, you wonder? Perhaps, Hannan, with so little to lose, would have had to work three times harder than her friend with much more to lose. This might be true, but still, if she'd done what Ronda had done, she could have lost more. *Two ladies, same diet, completely different results.* Women everywhere know the story of that one. The difference between the two lays in the pudding, or rather the cabbage soup.

Ronda's goal (also known as 'mini vision') had her seeing white. That is, she was engaged to be married and she wanted to look like the svelte bride in the most beautiful gown that her mother had kept for her all these years. Two months ago, the gown she'd lovingly dreamt of getting married in, even as a young girl, wouldn't go over her head. She couldn't imagine getting married in anything but it. And if the decision came between not getting married and losing 40 pounds, well she'd just have to lose the weight.

That is what you call purpose.

Hannan thought it would be nice to lose 10 pounds so she could eat as much cheesecake as she wanted without feeling guilty. But, if truth be told, last week (in between bowls of cabbage soup) she had stopped by the deli and had a slice of her favorite kind – the one with cherry pie filling on top. She swears it was an automatic instinct, that she didn't even realize she was cheating on her diet until after the last bite had been swallowed. Plus, Hannan insists, she was disciplined for the entire next day.

That is what you call NOT purpose.

And that, my dear queens of Sheba, is the difference

between a vision with staying power and one with so little steam that it can barely be called a blip on the screen, yet alone a vision.

Purpose, purpose, purpose.

It's interesting how when we are children, purpose is given to us by those that take care of us; our parents, our teachers, our friends, even our enemies play a role. If you've ever been bullied on a school playground because your pants were an awful brown color and didn't fit nice, you'll know what I mean about our enemies (but I did stand up to them, by the way). In childhood we don't reflect on why we do what we do, we just do. We are obedient because our parents expect it. We do our homework because our teachers grade it. We don't think about why we do things because we are just kids. But then we 'come of age' and start asking lots of why questions.

If those why questions have a readily available answer in the form of "...because, it supports the vision I have for my life (see chapter 8)," then we've found the missing link that will catapult our motivation.

Why do I want what I want? Why do I need to realize my particular vision? Why do I want to be the best queen of Sheba? Getting the answers to those why questions doesn't have to be a difficult task. The hard part is finding a vision that you care enough about to make this part of the process easy. If you haven't found that, then you definitely need to go back to the last chapter.

The best way to align your vision and your purpose is to really take stock of your values and hopes for your life. Recognizing what's important to you and drawing the associations that will move the vision forward lies in having the needs you care about most being met. It's about falling in love with the purpose behind your vision because the vision itself is in alignment with the values that you hold dear, the ones that you're passionate about and are already in love with. *Purpose. It's the queen's a posteriori.*

Protocol 9

Part one of this book was about learning who you are, making your confidence work for you, and discovering how to harness your thoughts to your advantage. The protocols were designed to put you in touch with what is strong and wonderful about you. In this chapter's protocol, I hope you can build on that knowledge in order to answer these crucial "why" questions in regard to your vision.

To start, please circle the top 3 things that matter to you most in the following list of words:

health, spirituality, family, friends, travel, excitement, money, security, knowledge, creativity, power, recognition, peace, balance, helping others

Can you think of others that aren't listed? Add them too. After you've really thought of why you chose the ones you chose, take out your journal and answer:

1. Why do I want to see this vision come to be?
2. Why is this vision my mission in this life?

Truly and deeply think about your answers.

Imagine someone you truly admire asking you these questions. How would you articulate the purpose behind your vision to the object of your admiration? Write that person a little speech about your purpose – and read it out loud as if that person can hear what you have to say. If the speech touches you to the very core of your being and you feel a sense of complete and utter euphoria about WHY you MUST pursue your vision, then by golly, I think you've got it! The queen has her purpose.

10

Is that Wonder Woman pretending to be the queen of Sheba?

After restricting herself to some lousy diet that she saw no purpose in adhering to, Hannan realized that going to the all ladies gym near her house could be a suitable alternative. This felt more doable. She'd always been a fan of sports - actually thought of taking up tennis at one point in her childhood. But first school and then her career had gotten in the way and she'd developed this bad habit of flopping down in front of the television and watching active people on TV.

Her habit of doing this directly after she came home from work (a stressful position teaching pre-teens) for hours while she consistently munched on unhealthy foods was draining on her. She'd decided enough was enough and this time her purpose was strong enough. She knew that spending an hour in the gym at least four nights a week would give her energy and clear her mind. She knew that she wanted to feel strong and healthy and that working out would make her feel happy. Most importantly, she really wanted to get involved in an annual run for cancer that some local sisters were organizing a group for. This run was important to her because her mom had died from breast cancer and part of Hannan's ultimate vision was to be a part of the cancer solution. Finally, on top of Hannan's personal values list was having the ability to help others and having good health and vitality came in there as well. Indeed, she had all her bases covered, and it promised to be a homerun.

Because her vision and purpose were in line, and after she made the commitment, it was fairly easy for Hannan to get to the gym. Her workouts weren't the very strenuous kind - usually just a mild walk on the treadmill or thirty minutes on the recumbent bike. One of the trainers encouraged her to step it up after assessing Hannan's goal to participate in the cancer run (a 10k feat). It was coming up, and Hannan had been telling herself that she'd gradually work up to harder workouts as she built her endurance. But instead of that happening, after 4 weeks of working out, her feet started to drag and it was becoming increasingly difficult to even make it to the gym, yet alone intensify the time spent exercising.

It happens. Complacency, routine, lack of focus, the inability to see the greater purpose, all work to sabotage even the most motivated amongst us. We'll be dealing with how to deal with hurdles more so later, but for the purpose of illustrating the function behind this protocol, I've included 'what happens' here. I should make clear that it is not necessary to experience a set-back in order to use this one. In fact, this chapter illustrates a powerful strategy for fulfilling your life's ultimate vision and it should carry you through as you work to make it happen.

It's the "pretend you're someone else" approach, also known as "fake it till you make it." It's about the roles you embrace as you work towards your goals. When you've defined your vision and connected with the purpose behind your vision, getting clarity on who you will be as the executor of said vision can be as easy as giving yourself a nickname. Or if it's to your liking (hopefully it already is), you take on the "I am Sheba" mantra. In fact, it may very well be that the entire concept of "release your inner queen of Sheba" finds its roots in this most important of tools. This is because it allows you to start to step away from the limitations and assume the possibilities.

To illustrate, consider some self-talk Hannan would use to convince herself to up the ante on her workouts: *"Come on Hannan, look at you. You really need to get out from in front of the TV and go to the gym. And Hannan, you should really go for a tougher workout this time. I know that you aren't used to strenuous activity, but you can do it, Hannan. Go, Hannan."*

I'm rolling my eyes. Are you? This self-talk simply is not convincing and frankly, I'm thinking that Hannan is probably rolling her eyes as she says it to herself too.

But consider what would happen if Hannan, in order to go forward in her desire for a tough workout, steps out of her Hannan persona and imagines (plays a very convincing game of pretend) herself to be Hannan Williams, the third sister, seeded to be the next all star tennis champion of the world. She has to train hard. She has to train fast. Hannan has marathons to run. She has prizes to win. She has to conquer cancer. She is not Hannan, stressed out public school teacher with an inviting television. She is Hannan, tennis champion training for an important race!

Now, which Hannan has a better chance of getting in a great workout?

Stepping into roles that will propel us forward is a sure-fire way to get in the right frame of mind to achieve. Who knows what athletes, politicians, or even actors tell themselves or who they 'become' in order to get into that "zone" of heightened performance. Some have been documented, such as the American football player who calls himself 'the beast' and his job is to tackle players from the opposing side. There is the wannabe starlet who says she is "channeling the ghost of Marilyn Monroe." There is the sister who volunteers at a shelter for the homeless and refers to herself as 'the catalyst'. There is the other sister who works as a pediatrician and when she's doing the rounds through the children's ward, likes to think she's 'Mr. Noodle,' the Sesame Street character, and her inner thoughts really reflect on her outward behavior. Even the sickest young patients recognize who she is and laugh so heartily that it brings sunshine to their days and her days too. There is the sister with a humdrum marital situation who names herself 'Aisha' in hopes of inspiring more fun-loving interactions with her husband. She thinks of the races Aisha, may Allah be pleased with her, would have with the prophet Muhammad, peace be upon him, and the lively conversations the two had together.

Islamic history describes how Ali, may Allah be pleased with him, the cousin of the Prophet Muhammad, peace and blessings be upon him, used to put himself into a certain 'zone' and say, *"I am the one whose mother named him the lion."* And by declaring this, he made his movements during battles fierce and decisive, and victory would be on his side.

I wonder what Wonder Woman was telling herself?

Protocol 10

In considering your vision and purpose, what wonderful role(s) will you embrace to help you realize it? What rousing nicknames or personas will inspire you?

Come up with a few ideas and choose the ones that you think can apply to the situations where you really need to take action, the situations that will bring you closer to that ultimate vision that you've painted for your life.

Really sit with the 'alter-egos' until you find the ones that hit a deep chord, the ones that make you want to jump. The more the persona resonates with you, the stronger the emotional attachment, the more useful it will be. This is when you need to trust your instincts, because they will guide you on what will work best for you. And what works best for you is what will work best for you.

Decide when the role will be most useful and visualize calling on it and stepping into it during those times, especially as they move you forward in your vision.

Now, articulate the details - who, what, where, and when of your role-playing in your journal. And start practicing, because practice makes perfect. How do you think Wonder woman was able to handle that lasso with such skill?

11

The

Burgeoning Queen

I am currently in the middle of three very engrossing books on three very relevant subjects. I won't give you the specific titles, but I'll tell you this much: one is concerned with the art of communication, the second is about website design, and the third is about great parenting. Why do you think I've chosen to read up about these subjects? It's because I've deemed these areas to be ones I need to work on as I move to realizing my visions and aspirations.

When we figure the what and the why, it's time to focus on the how. And when we take a look at areas we're lacking in as we work to achieve our visions, we can know what needs to be done in order to achieve them.

Consider Hind, a young woman who dreams of becoming a Muslim scholar. She is solid on why she wants to do this, and can even put herself in a state of "I'm the daughter of Aisha, the first female scholar of Islam". Next up for Hind is learning what she needs to learn in order to accomplish her mission.

In terms of doing what comes naturally (as expounded on in Part 1 of the book), working on areas that don't come naturally in this protocol isn't a contradiction. This is about finding areas that you need to see measurable results in because they are so crucial to making you realize your potential. This is about recognizing that castles are built with engineers who've studied the mathematics of it, and with a foundation of actual bricks; yes, the heavy kind. Not that the learning will be heavy, in fact, if you've done the previous protocols and found them enlightening, this type of learning will be most pleasurable because you are the engineer of the vision.

Hind loved studying Islam, but so far, it had been a casual thing, if she was truthful with herself, she might even admit that it had become a social thing. Hanging out with the girls during religious seminars had been taking up more and more of her study time. She needed to work on making Islamic studies a serious priority. This was the biggest area she needed to work on, the number one area.

Area number two, Hind figured, was in the field of communication. She knew that as a scholar of Islam, she'd have to speak about the religion to others. She wasn't a shy one - but she tended to 'be all over the place' when trying to articulate her thoughts in a concise manner. What to do?

Area number three to work on, as Hind saw it, was in getting rid of her vices. She had a few bad habits that she knew were not conducive to the life of an Islamic scholar. She had to purge herself in order that Allah place blessings in her time and in her vocation so that she could greatly benefit the masses with her visionary, scholarly status. She needed to be a living example of righteousness as much as possible.

Hind took a hard, honest look and defined three areas she needed to work on. Now that's not to say those are the only things, and once she'd had them covered, everything would be perfect, but it's saying that as human beings, especially those working towards their best destinies, we need to constantly evaluate the places where we can stand to learn a thing or two. Our systems are rigged by our Maker to always seek out growth, because 'that which no longer grows, begins to die.' Remember that human need? Scientific study after scientific study proves this point.

Humans are learning creatures, and developing the ability to continually move and take on new brain challenges is a wonderful way to feed that hunger. Learning is something that makes our lives fuller and gives us perspective. Also, if we focus on the teachings that will allow us to move ahead with our visions, it makes the learning experience all the more relevant and enriching. It allows us to easily adapt to situations that arise in the pursuit of that higher purpose. Mastering the knowledge and skills that will help us achieve the vision gives us the confidence to believe that anything is possible and we are capable of achieving that 'anything.' The learning deepens our character and can even help us inspire others in the same way.

The burgeoning queen of Sheba is she who always wants to move forward, to enhance her knowledge and improve in her abilities. When choosing the areas to focus on in order to realize your vision, it's important to step out of your comfort zone - at least a little bit. If Hind had already mastered the knowledge of the Islamic law rulings on funerals, for example, actually specifying this as an area she needs to improve on in order to realize her dream of becoming a scholar would be redundant and may even be a sign that her dream lacks purpose for her and a disconnect between what she really wants and what she says she wants.

When you are wholeheartedly passionate about the vision and the purpose, you'll easily find *the* areas that you need to work on. You'll work on those areas with fervor and excitement, perhaps even a bit of apprehension - think of a child's first day of school. You'll question if you can even do it. You'll wonder if you can learn to speak a new language in a few months, or train for a marathon when you've been inactive, but if it's not challenging, if it doesn't excite you, if you can't see how it will bring you closer to that vision you painted two protocols ago, then something needs to change.

This is not about hitting too many targets at once; it's about going for the gold in the specific categories that will allow you to move forward and realize your vision. It's about deciding the real areas you need to put your energy in so that the cycle of "I should do this and I should do that and I should do it tomorrow and you'd think that tomorrow should be coming but it doesn't ever seem to..." ends.

What begins is the desire to really learn what you need to in order to fulfill your vision and higher purpose.

Protocol 11

This protocol is about finding those areas that you are so keen to improve upon, that it's almost a feeling of desperation that fills you when you think about it. And when you do find them, you can't wait until tomorrow to get started. It is 3 o'clock in the morning, but you're determined to start your journey right NOW! If that means learning how to perfect an ice-sculpture for your catering business, you'll start filling up buckets of water to freeze and hunt for power tools in the garage, then you're doing it despite the early hour. That's the kind of zeal for learning I'm talking about.

The questions to answer in your journal are:

1. What three (you can choose less – but no more than five) areas am I crazy excited about, knowing that I MUST concentrate on and work towards improving on?
2. Why are these areas crucial to fulfilling my vision?
3. When and how will I start the learning?

12

"Well, aren't you the resourceful queen?"

If you are old enough to remember the action series that was a staple in the 80's called MacGyver, then you'll know exactly what the term 'resourceful' can signify. If you haven't a clue what I'm talking about, then what's stopping you from finding out right now?

Whether or not you know who MacGyver is, just pretend that you do not know but really had to find out. How would you learn more about him? Could you use internet search engines? That's certainly one way, but what if your internet access was disabled (for whatever reason), and you really need to find out now? Is there another resource you might use? Could you go to the library and look it up in a reference book? Could you ask someone who might have knowledge of it? Could you enroll for a class on TV history at a nearby community college?

You can certainly do any or all of these things and the more you can think of the different resources available to you and which one would be more helpful to your purpose, the more flexibility you can learn, and the more like MacGyver you can become. And you don't even need a Swiss Army Knife. Knowing what's out there and what or who can help you learn what you need to learn or do what you need to do is having the tangible resources to follow through with what you've deemed your life vision to be.

There are two parts to the equation when it comes to releasing your inner 'resourceful' queen. Part one entails developing you 'inventiveness muscles,' or the ability to think on your feet in circumstances that make you feel boxed in, that there is more than one way to get something done. Part two has you becoming aware of the actual resources, the tangible tools that are available to you. Both parts come together beautifully to make for one very resourceful queen.

Typically speaking, resources available to you as you pursue your vision may include books, classes, mentors, and support groups that are designed to help you. If we refer back to Hannan's specific vision to run that marathon, resources available to her are a trainer in the gym, an online forum on nutritional needs, and a motivational CD she bought recently. So far, the resources have been working well for her and the progress she's been making is wonderful.

But what happens if the trainer that she's been working with suddenly moves to Hawaii or learns she is pregnant and decides to go on early maternity leave? Hannan tries in vain to find a trainer to replace the old one but disappointment is beginning to set in. This is where Hannan must use her resourcefulness to find an alternate resource. Does the gym offer specific classes? Can she team up with a buddy that will motivate her to keep working at it? If she's completed part one of this book successfully, she's likely developed a working knowledge of who she is and what will motivate and inspire her most to keep going, so much so that realizing now which resource is most likely to benefit her should be an easy task.

Accessing what is available to us has never been easier. We just have to use some flexibility when it comes to incorporating the tools to our advantage. It's helpful to create a resource 'toolbox' to fall back on whenever we need to move forward. This toolbox should be organized in a meticulous manner, but at the same time, it should be really full. Filling it is a continuous process. As you move along in your life, some 'tools' may be dismissed because of their past failures, others may take centre-stage as the 'no fail' options, and still others may become inconsequential.

The point is that the toolbox should be ever evolving and the best manner in which to make it so is in the writer's favorite tool, the "brainstorm."

When I was in the fifth grade, my teacher loved the "brainstorm." The class would brainstorm everything from writing assignments to what to do for a sick classmate to bathroom pass rules and regulations. The ideas that would pour out of the 'allowed to roam free- thinking' minds of 10 year olds ranged from the insane to the brilliant, and everything in between. The teacher would be rushing to write it all down on the blackboard as the students blurted out their ideas for a set amount of time. She would write quickly, not discriminating or filtering anything someone blurted out (unless it was vulgar). It was fascinating to watch her go, the way in which she would rush to keep up with the ideas escaping from the students. It was as if a bag of marbles had been poured out onto the ground and she was frantic to gather them. And she literally had to put a cap on the outpouring as the time on the clock ran out. Then, she'd turn to look at us. Now that I think about it, she was probably just trying to catch her breath, but to my fifth grader self, the dramatic pause was very, well, dramatic. Every time she did it.

Finally, she would announce, "now, we see how it all fits together." Similar ideas were grouped together by different colored chalk and a student 'secretary' kept all the notes. Ideas that didn't seem to belong were erased and categories began to become clear. Ideas fit together, like a systematic map that was coming together almost magically.

Today, I think that brainstorming is called 'mind-mapping,' and learning how to do it well is probably one of the most useful tools an aspiring queen of Sheba will possess because not only can it be a spectacular strategy in times when she is feeling like she has no options, but also because it will define the specific resources that she can use now in order to get what she wants.

Protocol 12

1. Set an alarm timer to go off in 15 minutes.

2. Grab a pen and paper (not necessarily your journal) and at the very top of the page, write down:

Resources to Help me Achieve my Vision

3. Don't stop writing. Don't censor what you write at this stage. If you suddenly think – *'my cat can help me memorize Quran,'* don't question it, just write it down. Don't try to explain it or rationalize the idea and why it might work, just write it down.

4. The pen should not leave the paper for the entire 15 minutes. Go, go, go, just like my fifth grade teacher did with the class.

5. Once the timer has gone off, stop and take stock.

6. Do you recognize patterns? How about items that stand out as something you can really use and that may be particularly helpful? Are there resources that seem like they can work well together? Consider the ones that you haven't thought of before with a new perspective. What makes them special? Begin to visually group together the ones that jump off the page.

7. Once you've determined the resources that can help you the most, pull out your journal and compose 3 short paragraphs describing the 3 most promising ones and why you know that they would work to achieve your vision.

How excited are you now? If you're really feeling the energy and thinking "I can't wait to get started on this!" then you've found it. The resources you determine to be necessary in your pursuit should allow you a measure of excitement the likes of which you've never before been privy to experience. In other words, just underline this one sentence as a reminder: The way in which you pursue the vision should be as yummy as the vision.

13

Goooaaalll!

The queen of Sheba scores!

If there is one category the world of self-help does not have a shortage of, it must be the amount of goal-setting quotations out there. A quick online search would reveal a host of clichés and sayings. You've probably heard of many of them. But the power of a good quote is not in how good it sounds or how often it is repeated mindlessly. Its power is in its ability to move you and inspire you to take action.

If, from the start, I had bombarded you with such quotations or put the protocol you'll be following later in this chapter at the beginning of the book, I have a strong suspicion that I would have lost you early on. This book might have become a compilation of things you could probably read anywhere else, and is likely to be readily available in the psyches of the common woman who has heard that, *'she can do anything,'* or *'we're only limited by the limitations we set for ourselves,'* or *'set it and you'll get it.'* I resisted because in all likelihood, it would not have moved and inspired you to take real and lasting action. I waited, because I've seen the results (or lack thereof) in women before, and you probably have to. *Release Your Inner Queen of Sheba!* is a process, and I think that that is the beauty of it.

Consider Maisa who is desperate to put her life into 'high achievement mode' immediately! She seriously has to get something done and she has to get it done fast! So she seeks the help of a life coach. She may find one who will (proverbially)'kick her butt.' Perhaps, she'll get one that gives her assignments to do, all the while encouraging her and telling her that she can indeed do them. Or she may find a coach, who, for whatever reason, isn't able to match her energy, and in effect, makes Maisa feel like a 'deflated tire.' I'm not certain that any of these scenarios are good for Maisa, and even if one or the other offers her benefit, my guess is that it would be of the temporary variety. Real change, real awakening, real acceptance of who you are and what you are capable of, and real achievement, is a process. It is not necessarily a long process, but a process nonetheless. And that's why I waited for the second to last protocol in the second to last part of the book to put it into play.

To set goals, you have to know who you are and what you are good at (seven protocols in part one to establish this). To set goals, you have to know what you want, why you want it, and how you are going to get it, (last five protocols to hammer in this one). Now, I think, I hope and I pray that you are ready to set those goals. And, the great thing about coming this far, having completed the protocols with flying colors means that you are indeed ready to set those goals and make them relevant ones, make them the kind with staying power.

For Maisa, that means she really has to go on a journey of self discovery. She has to sit with herself and begin to get in touch with why things haven't always gone her way, why she procrastinates things that she knows she 'should' do, and why the cycle of motivation, deflation, and subsequent feelings of failure, continually rotate in her life. They rotate in that order, over and over again. For Maisa, the bigger problem lies in the fact that once she sets goals that she ultimately fails to accomplish, the goals (and dreams) move further away from her sights. She keeps lowering her standards, thinking that that may be the solution - but instead, it makes her feel worse because, somewhere deep within her soul, she knows she can do better. She knows she is capable of more.

The first step for Maisa is to follow the previous twelve

protocols, but since you are not Maisa and *you've* already done that, then you're in the right place here.

So, how do you set goals?

SMART Goals
Perhaps you've heard of the SMART mnemonic. While there are a few different takes on what each letter stands for, SMART is usually referred to as:

- **S** Specific
- **M** Measurable
- **A** Attainable
- **R** Relevant or realistic
- **T** Time-bound

These are standards by which to measure the attainability of the goal. So, for example, instead of setting a goal like "I want to memorize some Quran", you'd make the standard more SMART by articulating the goal as, "I will memorize Chapter 2, Surah Albaqarah on (insert specific date) and for every week that passes along in this journey, I will have studied ten verses so deeply that I will know them like I know my own name. Yes, I am Sheba!"

The more precise you are with the dates, times, and amounts needed to realize the goal, the more you can measure your achievement towards it. If Hannan's goal was to lose 2 pounds of fat and gain 3 lbs of lean muscle mass (yes, I'm pretending to know what 'lean muscle mass' means) by the end of the month, and half way through, she's only lost .75 pounds and gained 1 pound of lean muscle mass, then she'll recognize that she's falling short, and begin to make some changes. Alternatively, come mid-month, Hannan may realize that she is in fact, ahead of the goal and decide to splurge on a chocolate sundae with whipping cream and a cherry on top. The point is that if she's declared her goal with these precise guidelines, she'll know when she gets there.

It's also imperative that you set priorities when you have goals. This ensures that you aren't overwhelmed with the goals that you're trying to balance. As you go through the protocol below, you'll realize that it's imperative to stick to the ultimate vision and your higher purpose. If you state goals that you can't connect to these, and ones where the resources you've deemed necessary to your success aren't utilized, then you may indeed lose your focus and feel overwhelmed. A disconnect might factor in, and you *don't* want that to happen.

Also, it's important that you take great care so that the goals you do set are ones in which you are the executor of them. Not your husband, not your mom, and not the boss in whose hands your salary increase lies. You do this by making your goals ones that are driven by your drive, your passion, your vision. *You* have to do the work. And if the goals reflect this, then you're good and ready.

When setting your goals, make certain that they stress your own personal performance, because that way, you retain control over them. If something goes wrong, you know what changes need to be made for next time. If something goes right, then there is no sweeter satisfaction than when a queen scores!

Protocol 13

In your journal, set the following (making sure that the goals are aligned with your set vision and purpose):

My SMART goals for the next year are:
My SMART goals for the next 90 days are:
My SMART goals for the next 30 days are:
Next week, I will have achieved these SMART goals:
TODAY: I will take these 2 steps to start on these goals:

14

Lifting it up

$\mathcal{I}$t is time for a reality check. The last six protocols have probably had you feeling like you can do anything you set your mind to. Maybe you've already started to accomplish the impossible. Maybe you've finally convinced yourself that you can be, do and have all that you've ever dreamt possible. Maybe you feel as if the world is your oyster.

Well, it isn't. The world can be one great big lonely place. And have you eaten an oyster lately? They really don't taste all that good.

Huh? What kind of supposed motivator speaks nonsense like this, you wonder? Why, when I've promoted hope and the awakening of a powerful purpose within you, am I now pulling away the rug from beneath you?

I'm doing this because now is the time when you need to realize that as lofty as your vision is, there is One who is loftier. As strong as your purpose is, there is One who is stronger. And as generous as your goals are, there is One who is more generous. That One is Allah.

As you have moved along in the process of releasing your inner queen of Sheba, you may have asked yourself if you're doing things that would be pleasing to Him. You may have wondered how your relationship with Him should be in relation to this process. You may have already drawn nearer to Him. But perhaps, in the 'business' of it, you've let it slide a bit.

This is the last protocol in part two and before we move on, I really wanted you to get a ringing endorsement from Allah. Hopefully, if you do get this endorsement, it can be the final push that will have you trusting completely in who you are and what you've deemed your life's mission to be. This endorsement will be the saving grace when you begin to face the hurdles, because you will face them. This endorsement will be a voice deep within in you that will trust - even as your mind seems ready to forsake. This endorsement will be the one that will allow you to make decisions easily and without regret. Yes, I said, "without regret. "Once you get this endorsement, nothing you do will be wasted, nothing you fail to accomplish, a failure. With this endorsement, everything you do will be successful, every experience a chance to grow, and every moment, an opportunity. If you were sure that you would never regret a decision, what would you do with your life?

Jabir ibn Abdullah, may Allah be well pleased with him, said: "Allah's Messenger (peace be upon him) used to teach us how to seek guidance in choosing the best option available in practical matters, just as he would teach us chapters from the Quran. If one of you is concerned about some practical undertaking, or about making plans for a journey, he should perform two cycles of ritual prayer, not as obligatory observance, but voluntarily. Then he should say: *'O Allah, I ask You to show me what is best, through Your knowledge, and I ask You to empower me, through Your power, and I beg You to grant me Your tremendous favor, for You have power, while I am without power, and You have knowledge, while I am without knowledge, and You are the One who knows all things invisible. O Allah, if You know that this undertaking is in the best interests of my religion, my life in this world, and my life in the hereafter, and can yield successful results in both the short term and the long term, then make it possible for me and make it easy for me, and then bless me in it. O Allah, if You know that this undertaking is NOT in the best interests of my religion, my life in this world, and my life in the hereafter, then turn it away from me, and make it easy for me to do well, wherever I may happen to be, and make me content with Your verdict, O most Merciful of the merciful."*

Also known as 'istikhara' in Arabic, the strength of the supplication lies in the humility of the one who seeks the guidance of his or her creator. Now, many will pray it dutifully when making big decisions. They may wait for a dream to come to them or some sort of sign that would show them without doubt what it is that they should do. And indeed that sign may come in a very tangible form. I've heard countless stories of this from very reliable people, and have witnessed it myself on more than one occasion. And yet, on other occasions, the answers you're looking for may not be entirely tangible. And this is precisely when you have to start trusting.

You need to start trusting in your maker, in His infinite endowments to you. You need to start trusting in your gut, your heart, and mind, because they will know the answers, by His will. We're able to start listening when we begin to trust that HE, too, is listening. And once we can believe that completely, we can become unstoppable, no matter what "unstoppable" may mean.

There was this one week last summer that was a true testament to this fact for me. I had been working on the first draft of this very book for over six months when my computer crashed. I had absolutely no back up of it - and the entire draft was lost. I remember people close to me had kept on telling me that I should save my work somewhere, but somehow, I didn't listen. *And I'm glad that I didn't listen.* I'm glad that I didn't listen because that first draft was meant to go. The Monday that I awoke to work only to find that the inevitable had happened, I remember feeling a real sense of calm. "It's all right, there's nothing on my computer that I'm going to miss," I heard myself say to the concerned members of my family, who lamented on the work lost.

I remember feeling that I definitely needed to go out and buy a new computer immediately because I had much work to do. No, I wasn't in denial, but I was acutely aware, and kept hearing my gut tell me that, *"Allah wants me to do better."* And as I've toiled to complete this version, I can honestly say that I can't even remember anything from that lost version. And I think, and I hope you'll agree with me, but most importantly, I pray that Allah is pleased with this version more so than the one that is gone.

There were other signs that week as well. There was the sister who had an incredible monetary windfall - paying off a debt that was beyond imaginable. There was the brother who was able to bring Islam to the heart of a dying grandmother who'd long fought with him over it. There was the mother who realized that the situation she was currently in would destroy her relationship with Allah and committed to making a radical change that has her, for the first time in her life, realizing what being a Muslim really means. Each one of us that week spoke a different story, but there was a common thread. We had taken it upon themselves to "life it up", to make sincere supplication to Allah and TRUST that He would hear us.

So often we pray for things because, well, just because. I hate to say it, but I think that we pray from a place of vanity. We want - we want - we hear that Allah gives and so we give it a shot. But, what if we could grow so that our prayers come from a place of complete surrender? You've lifted it up when you ask of your Maker – you've put what it is that you want in His capable hands and you trust that He, knows best and, no matter what, He will answer.

Aisha, may Allah be pleased with her, said: "No believer makes a supplication to Allah and it is wasted. Either it is granted here in this world or deposited for him in the Hereafter as long as he does not get frustrated."

Allah the exalted, has said, *"Pray unto me and I will hear your prayer"* (Quran 40: 60) and *"Call upon your Lord with humility and in private"* (Quran 7:55) and *"When My servants question thee concerning Me, I am indeed close (to them): I listen to the prayer of every supplicant when he calls on Me."* (Quran 2: 186)

So you start praying, and you start working, and you work for what you are praying for. And now that you've found your goals you know what it is your praying for and you know what it is that you're working for. Someone once said, "work as if everything depends on you, pray as if everything depends on God." Because it does.

Protocol 14

Your mission is to pray the istikhara prayer as described above. Have it geared towards the goals you've set out in the last protocols. When you're done, ask yourself how good you feel about your vision and aspirations now? Does your heart feel open and warm? Did you get your sign?

If yes, and all lights are green, and you completely feel that everything is working to make this vision happen, proceed. This is your ringing endorsement.

If not, ask yourself why not? Does something need to change? It's imperative that you seek Allah's guidance and that you keep praying for trust. And 'trust' is a good key word.

Part Three

If all lights are green. But as you're driving, the lights won't always be green, will they? Sometimes, you can see the red ones from a distance away. Other times, you get the warning yellow color that tells you to slow down. And then there are the times when you see yellow and you hesitate. Should you go for it? Or should you wait? Can you clear the intersection? Or will you be stuck in a sticky situation?

Driving can be such a finicky thing. Most new drivers are of the cautious variety; they can hesitate, and miss out on opportunities. Would it surprise you to know that many older drivers who've been driving for years can be the same? Some new drivers may be more daring. Despite their lack of driving experience, they'll think instinctively, "I can make it – I'll clear the intersection." And some older ones may be the same, they might say, "I've been through enough yellow lights in my life to recognize how long I have before it turns red." Who is right and who is wrong is not the issue. The issue is not even about whether or not you'll crash your car or save your life from a potential crash. It's about the keyword, trust. Some learn to trust their instincts early on the road, others go through a lifetime without finding the ability to do so. The funny thing is that that ability was always so near.

In the last protocol, it was about trusting your creator.

And when you're able to trust HIM, then trusting yourself has to happen next.

What do you give to a man who literally has everything? When the magnificent gifts of Bilqis were returned to her by Solomon, peace be upon him, she knew that she would have to go, to meet face to face with this very persuasive prophet and see what he had to say. And so she went. As she embarked on her journey, Solomon looked around his host and asked: who can bring me her throne?

One very smart jinn with knowledge of the Book retorted that he could bring it to Solomon before he blinked his eyes. And so, even as she made the trip, the throne of Bilqis found itself in a new home. When she entered his magnificent lands, the Queen of Sheba found herself dazzled. It was unlike anything she'd seen before (and she'd seen much) - but she held her composure. Solomon, in his first act of welcoming Bilqis, brought forth her throne and questioned her, asking "is this your throne?"

Now, a queen knows what her throne looks like, no doubt, but she stalled. How was it humanely possible that this could be her throne? There was one route from Saba and her kingdom to that of Solomon. If someone had robbed her palace in order to steal her throne and present it to Solomon, surely she would have seen the thief on route.

So, she replied, "it is as if it is." I love that answer! She didn't confess or cry, "what have you done!" She stood her ground, while remaining present and aware. There is no doubt that it was the smartest answer. But, Solomon, undeterred, was a man on a mission. He wanted to show the queen that he was a messenger from Allah and that it was not benefitting for her to take the sun as her lord. And he knew that to win her over would mean that her people and entire kingdom would return to the worship of the one and only God. And so he took her to his 'sarh' - which has been described as a magical glass floor that looked like a body of water. Bilqis, deceived by the semblance of water, lifted her skirts and was astonished when she realized the floor was not a wet one. Finally, her doubts and fears were squelched and she surrendered. *"She said: O my Lord! I have indeed wronged my soul: I submit, with Solomon, to the Lord of the universe."* *(Quran 27:44)*

And that my dear sisters, is the essence of this last part of the process. Surrender. You've learned who you are, you've set goals and aspirations for yourself, and now comes the part where you are in tune to what is right for you.

In this part you'll learn how to take the challenges and rise above. Trust that you will. You'll learn to banish any negative thoughts that hold you back and sabotage your lifelong pursuit of releasing your inner queen of Sheba. Trust that you will. Perhaps, most importantly, you'll learn how to be happy with the process. Trust that you will. You'll learn how to be authentically happy with everything you do and everything that comes your way - forever and for always, no matter what. Trust that you will. In that trust and in surrendering it all, you'll learn the most important lesson of all. It's good to be queen.

15

It's good to be queen!

*C*old and Colder. Movies could be made about how cold Winnipeg, Canada, is. In fact, I think it's the 'hot spot' (literal joke) for Hollywood films set in the ice age. Winter starts sometime in late September and ends in late June. And then July and August are just for the local folks to get a breather - a taste of what others experience. Seriously, it is cold.

Although, I'm willing to concede that global warming might have done a number on the climate there now, when I was growing up, this is what I experienced. You could literally feel your flesh freezing beneath layers of heavy clothing, and for the life of me, I could never find a pair of boots that would keep the ends of my toes warm. Just thinking about it now makes me want to grab a thick blanket and snuggle inside and as I'm writing this – it's a warm summer day.

I detest air conditioners and always want the heat on full blast. My children think I'm crazy when I do this, but when I explain my days in Winterpeg (commonly named by its citizens, commonly - not lovingly) in those days of extreme weather and how no matter what you did, the cold seemed to touch your very core and you couldn't get warm enough, they try and understand. Still, they'll open windows when I'm not looking. But, I get it, *they are* experiencing the weather as it is.

Maybe it's because I was born in Egypt, the sun's warmth runs in my veins and I always seek it out. Then again, my mother is Egyptian too, and back then she was new to the cold as well, and even she thought that I had some sort of wiring problem.

"Heba, get your feet away from me!" she'd admonish as we lay underneath the blankets on Sunday afternoons. I loved this time. I had no school. She was off from work. And 'lazy-day Sunday' became a ritual. We'd stretch out, talk, laugh, and enjoy it utterly. My mom and me.

From then I learned that no matter how cold, how hard, or how 'anything' your life becomes, there is always the day you carve out where you allow yourself a bit of "laziness." You stop working, you stop walking to school in boots that act like slippers, you stop wondering about what good it would all amount to, and you revel in the simple joy of letting go. And the knowledge that if you were to finish the week, another lazy-day Sunday would be yours would be enough to keep you going from one week to the next. It would be your time to do whatever. Slack off, read a book, enjoy a cup of herbal tea and day dream about a vacation under a sweltering sun.

Honestly, this is a habit that could end up being one of the best things that you can do for yourself. Not only will it help you to physically relax, reducing your heart rate and blood pressure, and any other sort of anxiety, but it also allows you the atmosphere to think about things more peacefully and more creatively. They say Winnipeg was a 'hotbed' (another literal joke) for artists and writers. I think it has to do with the fact that they were so cold that they had to have had those "trying to keep warm under the blankets" lazy days too.

Dedicated "it's good to be queen time" is beneficial on so many levels. Here are a few that sisters have reported:

1. It helps get you ready for a big event. "If I had a party coming up, I could imagine the food that people would fill their plates with, see the way the house was cleaned and decorated, picture what a gracious host I would be," says Rabiah. Similarly, this time can help you prepare for any big event by visualizing how much of a smash hit you're going to be. Planning a wedding? Having a big job interview? Just daydream about how wonderfully it will all go, anticipate the process and take the time to prepare.

2. It helps you appreciate your reality. How truly wonderful is your guy? He smiles politely at your stinky morning breath and treats you like a shining star. How about the roses in your garden? Aren't those just the loveliest on the entire block? What are you grateful for? What is beautiful in your life? "Counting my blessings during this time," says Jehan, "makes me see the bigger picture, and I feel wonderful long after."

3. It helps you get to the bottom of what ails you. Imagine how you might have handled something a bit better. Did you have to yell at your son for spilling the milk? Perhaps you didn't have to take what your friend said so personally. She probably didn't mean it. This time can help you learn from your mistakes and come up with a plan for getting ahead.

4. It'll inspire you. The next big idea awaits you in your dedicated "it's good to be queen" session. It could be lines of poetry, or a business venture. Taking the time like this can connect you with your passion, your unique talents and the roads that can lead you to success.

I honestly believe, when setting a regular time for this, your thoughts will come from a better, more relaxed and peaceful place. So, go ahead, schedule some 'good to be queen time'. Do this for 21 times (once a week) until it becomes a ritual that you'll do years and years later. And this message is for my mom: *I love you for teaching me this one - and I especially love when we get to do it together.*

Protocol

You don't need a cold winter storm to sink yourself into this protocol. But I'm thinking of making that warm blanket mandatory. It's going to be called your "it's good to be queen time." And the benefits will amaze you.

Designate a day of the week that you can let all other responsibilities slide (or at least be put aside for a while). But, don't designate a particular time on that day – the timing should come naturally and joyfully whenever during that day you've designated as lazy. And there's no minimum time to worry about - just make sure that you are consciously 'staying under the blankets' for a time.

It's meant to be a most pleasurable experience. Really love it. Stretch, smile. Feel gratitude and joy in the moment. Feast in the moment. And just.... let your mind wander. Relax. Tune into your body and soul.

What's that you hear? Is it whispering to you?

16

The queen whisperer

*I*ve never read the book the "Horse Whisperer" by Nicholas Evans, but I do know that it became a pop culture phenomenon that introduced the masses to the idea that whispering isn't just something that you do in the library under the watchful eye (or ears) of a hard-nosed, old-school librarian. Rather, a whisperer emerged as someone who communicates on an entirely different level than typical humans. Today, you may have heard of the dog whisperer, the cart whisperer, or even the baby/ potty whisperer (a set of real books - no joke).

When we treat our minds and bodies with consideration and compassion, the connection between our thoughts and our actions (as well as our readiness to trust the two) becomes evident. We won't operate from a place of deprivation, hopelessness, or frustration (three things that can bring all our aspirations crashing down), or even fear. How many women lie awake at nights worried that their husband is going to leave or that the bills won't be paid or that a horrible disease might come to someone they love? What if we could banish those worries by learning to listen to what our minds and bodies need so that we can give it to them? How many sleepless nights could we save ourselves? How many mistakes could we prevent?

I'm completely convinced that becoming our own whisperers will not only spare us from the heartache that plagues other women, but it will also help us age gracefully and happily. Plus, we'll have some restful sleep. I'll tell you why I believe this because of my encounter with one extraordinary woman, but first, let me explain a bit further.

A whisperer's main duty is to make the object of its whispering feel like it can operate from a place of calm and trustworthiness. That operational mode might allow a horse to calm down or a baby to learn how to use the potty. The queen whisperer is the same. In essence, it's everything you've learned to this point. But it's also the ability to treat your mind and body so well that they will speak to you in order to let you know what they need. Plus, 'they' will become 'one'. Mind, spirit, heart, soul, body - all the elements will, Allah willing, work together so that even the smallest shift in harmony will be recognizable to you. And you'll instinctively know what to do about it.

By becoming your own whisperer, you'll learn to treat yourself right, so much so that you'll be tuned in to your moods so acutely that you'll be able to precisely pinpoint when a bout of anger or hopelessness or happiness or even a cold is coming on. You'll know how to nip negativity in the bud, and to deal with it in the right way - because you'll be operating from a place of "calmness" and positivity.

The benefits of becoming your own best whisperer can seep into all areas of your life, including your diet. You'll know to listen when your body says it wants salad instead of chocolate. Or chocolate instead of salad. Or if your bones are hurting, your body might ask for milk. A doctor's diagnosis may confirm that in fact you do have a calcium deficiency. At which point, you won't be surprised, because you've heard your body telling you the very same. You won't worry – "oh my, I'm going to get osteoporosis," and have this doom and gloom attitude that could make you sicker. You'll drink you milk, take you supplements and calmly do some weight bearing exercises because your body has told you that it's ready. And you listened.

Completely and fully becoming your own 'queen whisperer' is a process that might take years to develop (but the protocol strategies later are meant to start the 'tuning in' process). Indeed, I'm still working on it, but I've met a few women who seem to have it covered. One, in particular stands out in my mind.

She is the daughter of a well respected tribal leader - apparently they could trace their lineage to Amr ibn Al'Aas, the legendary companion of the prophet Muhammad (peace be upon him) who was most noted for his military leadership in the conquests of Egypt and North Africa. Not only for her noble status, this woman, is revered amongst the people in her village, for her advice and the power of her prayers. A sort of medicine woman, if you will - albeit, likely untrained, she gives people health advice, relationship advice, and health advice. She encourages her fellow villagers to always turn to Allah in supplication, and apparently she does this from the position of someone who is respected for own, one lady even told me that she felt this woman's prayers were a sign from Allah. There was the time when she prayed for 'so and so (a town gossip)' to be silenced. He was later diagnosed with throat cancer. There was the time when she prayed for rain after a particularly dry period, and it came instantaneously. And there was the time that she actually fell into a deep hole and was quickly rescued by a child who wanted to call for help but she prayed that Allah give him strength and he managed to get her out himself.

She isn't a wealthy woman, in fact, she's far from it. She refuses to accept any monetary compensation for the advice she dispenses. She's not had an easy life either. In fact, she had been divorced, virtually unheard of in her town and time. She married again, someone twice her age. And she had had her share of suffering too. She had buried three of her own children - one of which died when he was almost four years old.

I had heard this much and more, which I (admittedly) dismissed as 'uneducated village' myth. But I was looking forward to meeting her myself, and as you can probably imagine, it was a fascinating encounter. I didn't find some urban legend of a woman, but one who'd become her own queen whisperer (even though I hadn't put a name to it then).

When I finally sat down with her and her daughter, who now acts as her nurse, I was surprised to find a humble, generous, light hearted woman. She laughed at everything (my daughter's shyness, her daughter's jibes, her own jokes) throughout the day I spent there, and as people came in and out, I watched and realized that she really enjoyed the conversations she has with them. It didn't take much to get her talking about herself (I wasn't researching the book, just have a natural curiosity and I like to hear the stories of others) and even though she didn't really know me - she was completely open and forth coming. I smile on it now because even though I didn't understand it all (her Arabic is a tribal sect dialect that I'm not too familiar with - and she thought my Arabic was the "Pakistani version") - one concept came across loud and clear. This was a woman who was acutely "aware".

I asked her about the secrets of her prayer making powers - and she brushed it off.

"I've made many prayers," she smiles, "that I'm still waiting for Allah to answer. But at the same time, I'm completely sure that He will answer - even if I die before I see them answered."

She talked about how she realized she had arthritis when her bones started to feel 'cold'. She mentioned how she knew her young son was going to die when he looked her in the eyes days before he did. He had had a cough that her husband brushed off and refused to treat. She actually went behind his back to take the toddler to the lone hospital in the village, but nothing could be done for the boy. She told me about her divorce and how hard it should have been to deal with the cultural repercussions, but how Allah gave her piece of mind to not fall into a depression.

She tells me how after she got divorced, the town's people that had just been in her house asking for her advice had been so cruel at the time.

"Ahh, how people are fickle," she reflects. "I remember how they were ready to burn up my character at the time. They said that I was a whore, and lazy" (one of the worst things a woman can be in those parts – apparently, ugly is better than lazy). I want to ask how she found it in her heart to forgive them, let them in her house and listen to their needs, but she continues on before I get the chance.

"I wasn't lazy," she stresses, "I used to get all my work done before the household even woke up." I nod my head in understanding. Being a busy mother, I could relate to the necessity of getting things done while everyone else was sleeping. Plus, I'd heard others talk about how she was over 80, and despite the arthritis, and now diabetes, had a physical vitality that would rival someone half her age. Indeed, she doesn't look that old at all.

Perhaps my nod encourages her to explain further. I see that she hesitates, considering what she'll say next, wondering if I can be trusted. We're alone in the room now, and she leans in, and I feel like she's about to share something really deep with me.

"My mother-in-law was a devil!"

I almost laugh out loud, but sensing that it isn't a good time, I stifle it. I'm rewarded when she continues.

"She was crazy. In those days, things very different from today, the mother-in-law was your master - the husband, her puppet. Mine made my life miserable. She even beat me. And I had no option but to endure. She would lock me in a room at her whim. There was no TV then, and girls were not taught how to read. All I could do was pray to Allah during hose times, and the only companion I had in my room that had become my prison was myself. I learned to speak to myself like I was my own best friend.

I came to understand things so clearly - I knew that

Allah would find a way out for me. I couldn't see how it would be possible unless she died. But she actually went against all social norms and had her son divorce me. I learned to listen to my body - so that if my body craved a certain food that would speed up the healing process from her abuse, I would find ways to eat it. I learned to listen to my heart so that when it spoke to me saying that everything would be all right, I believed it. I didn't know in those times how the story would end, but I believed that it would be all right because I trusted that Allah would take care of me, and that I would survive."

I was awestruck, wanting desperately to hear more, but in a flash she backed away. Her daughter had entered the room carrying a tray with both hands, "time for your medicine," she told her mother.

"I feel my blood sugar is fine now," retorted the old woman. "Perhaps I'll need the medicine in a few hours. Right now, just give me the glass of water." She chugged at it readily and put it down with a grateful sigh. "For dinner, make me 'hassa' (a soup of whole grains)."

I watched as she then placed a cushion under her head and reclined her body on the sofa. It was late afternoon and time for her siesta. In less than a minute, she was snoring gently. Her daughter apologized and asked if I'd like to see how hassa was made.

"She knows exactly what she needs," I remarked and her daughter laughed. "Yes, and it means hard work for me. But I can't complain, you wouldn't believe how much housework she gets done before I even wake up!"

It dawned on me then that this woman wasn't some myth or legend, but one who'd learned (through whatever means that helped her learn it) to treat her body and mind right. She had learned to acutely listen and heed and establish a routine that worked for her. She operated from a place of calm and trust - and the more we can emulate that, the better our inner queen whispers will serve us.

Protocol 16

These exercises will help you to stop when your body says "NO!" but embrace ideas and thoughts that will have it jumping with "Yes, give me more of where that came from!" You've already started to take the 'good to be queen time,' and now we add to it.

First, I'd like you to take a day (or 21 days) to consciously treat yourself like a child who has confidence problems. Watch what you say and think at all times and then turn it around, so much so that you exaggerate the turn around. So, for example, if you think, *"I'm so fat, I need to go on a diet,"*- consciously counter with *"I'm not fat, I'm beautiful, and my body has served me well."* Lavish praise on your body, and soul, even if it feels like you are being ridiculous.

Just keep doing this for 21 days, and your body will start to respond. *"Yes, I have served you well. Do you see how rarely you get sick?"* Or, it might say something else. You just have to earn the trust and listen. And you'll see, just like a timid child who suddenly feels comfortable because of the teacher's kindness and starts to come out of his or her shell, so too will your body begin to speak to you.

Next, grab your journals and reflect on:

A) The most positive experiences of your life. What times were you feeling completely safe, secure, and positive? Describe them and what specifically was special about the effect they had on you.

B) How you'll treat your body and mind right. What new experiences will you allow yourself? What new projects will you undertake and what does your body think of them?

Your mind and body need to be challenged, to always move forward and gain an appreciation for what can be done. Maybe it wants to learn to knit? Maybe it needs to take an IQ test? Maybe it wants to travel to Winnipeg and do some skiing?

But, if that's the case than your body should know that because Winnipeg is flat prairie land, it'll have to be cross-country skiing. *Nothing is downhill from there, only the horizon is visible. You can see a body coming from a mile away.* And you can see exactly how much luggage she's carrying.

17

This queen

travels light

That was then. This is now. To me, it is the title of a novel studied in the seventh grade. To Firdaus, it is the mantra of her life. It's the affirmation she has repeated almost daily for the last seven years. That was about the time when she woke up and realized that she would no longer allow her past to interfere with her present and certainly not her future.

I sat down with her and she shared tidbits here and there - but nothing solid that I could begin to draw a complete picture from. Now, naturally, human beings can be curious - and I'm no exception. But as graciously as I could hint that I wanted to know more without appearing nosy, as firmly as Firdaus refused to spill the beans.

There were some tidbits that came out. She'd been hurt. Badly. By people who shouldn't have hurt her. She'd allowed the hurt to take over her life, dropping out of school, taking menial jobs to pay the bills, trusting no one. Hating herself. Thinking that she would never amount to anything. She was "ugly and stupid and very mad about it," she said. And if something good had come into her life, she wouldn't have recognized it. She allowed her fear of the past repeating itself to manifest itself in her daily actions and she pushed any possibility of goodness away. She ate and ate. She abused her body and her mind. She turned on the few friends that she did have so that she was utterly alone.

Thinking that she'd said too much, she turned on me, asking if I was some sort of therapist. I shook my head, asking instead, "do you think you need one?"

"Perhaps I did," she admitted, "but I'll be fine now. That was then. This is now."

Well, if she wouldn't describe what had happened to her, I wasn't about to let her go without at least telling me how it was that she'd managed to turn her situation around. When I insisted that she could help other women by sharing the secret, she conceded and said,

"I decided I needed to lose the baggage."

As simplistic as that sounded, it really resonated with me because I'd learned that lesson in the most literal of ways years before. My family and I had been traveling and my youngest son, who was two years old at the time, was quite the fussy one. Our carry on plane items included his stroller (one of the big, heavy kinds), a diaper bag, a few toys to keep him occupied, our own handbags - plus our two other children. It was a miserable flight, not only because all the 'stuff' failed to keep him quiet, but also because we were 'stuffed' in the middle of it all. An overhead compartment can only take so much.

When we disembarked (the last ones because we had to let everyone go first in order to not interrupt the line flow with our things, and also to avoid the nasty stares from people who knew the source of all that shrieking was my little boy), my husband realized that we'd forgotten the diaper bag underneath the seat. He left me with everything there at the gate, telling me to wait while he went back to retrieve it. As I stood there, juggling all the baggage, I put my son down and tried to open the stroller, thinking that if I could get him locked in, it would be better. So, there I was, fumbling with the stroller locks and almost as if in slow motion - I watched him run from me and start to slip between the gate opening and the plane's doors. There's a slight open space there that falls at least fifty feet to the concrete ground below. It's not big enough for a human being - but it would easily fit a two-year-old. I remember screaming and a savvy steward pulled my son back in the nick of time.

I'll never forget that painful, frightening moment and the lesson it taught me: Always, always, always, travel light. Struggling with the baggage you carry will not only dissuade you from enjoying the scenery, it can make you discard the important things and lose out on what matters.

Undoubtedly, emotional baggage can be harder to lose, because it lives in that which cannot be seen. It touches your existence on so many different levels. Not only can it impact your self-image and self-respect, but also you ability to deal with even the smallest of 'situations'. At its worst, emotional baggage can create havoc on your entire belief system. Constantly being in 'victim mode,' is a bad place to be, definitely not befitting of a queen of Sheba.

According to Firdaus, (and experts will agree) that when dealing with such issues, you have to contend with the pain of the baggage and the belief that you have no control over it, but that it has control over you. When Firdaus decided that she would lose the baggage, she knew that she would have to somehow find a way to forgive the person(s) who hurt her - not simply 'forget' about the hurt. She tried forgetting, she said, but it just didn't work. And forgiveness was something she completely resisted - something she felt that she could never do.

When she questioned why she couldn't forgive, it didn't take much to realize that it was a matter of dignity. She felt like if she were to forgive, it would be as if she was condoning the acts against her. It would be as if all her years of suffering as the victim would have been in vain.

One message that came at the right time in her life helped make the shift for her a much easier thing. Someone wise told her that forgiveness is actually a gift you give yourself. Forgiveness is not an act of compassion, but rather a selfish one because it frees you from the burden of responsibility that, for whatever absurd reason, keeps you chained to events that happened in the past and are done with. Forgiveness means that you can stop wasting time, energy, and money (therapy sessions don't come cheap) on futile resentment.

And when Firdaus understood that all her dreams and hopes for her future were vanishing before her very eyes - she realized that time is indeed of the essence. How much more of it could she waste on not living her life? Firdaus took a leap of faith, put down her baggage, and resolved to do her best never to pick it up again.

How could she be certain that she'd learned the lesson for life and that she would indeed refrain from burdening herself with the baggage again? She says that she feels like it just doesn't hurt anymore, that she keeps persevering and when she is down, she literally refuses to go back and play victim. She does this, she stresses, as vehemently as she refuses to fulfill my obvious curiosity.

That was then. This is now.

"Repetition of that mantra should be enough for your readers," she insists.

Protocol 17

Do you have baggage that needs to be unloaded? Here are the five steps that will hopefully set you free, but please note that some baggage can be difficult to unload and may require professional help.

Step 1: Identify what's inside your particular piece of baggage. Imagine yourself really ripping it open - see what's in the pockets and what's hiding between the socks. You've been lugging it around all this time, don't you at least deserve to see what it contains?

Step 2: Write down the reality of what you see on a piece of paper (not your journal). Really express the ugliness in the words that you use. Purge your soul on this paper (I hope that you don't need too much paper, but use as much as you need).

Step 3: Take out your journal and answer this question: What needs to happen in order for me to lose this piece of baggage forever?

Step 4: If you feel that your answer is wonderful, and completely something that you can do and may in fact be eagerly anticipating doing, then rejoice.

If you feel that your answer is too simple, and you think you might be doing this exercise wrong - I don't know, maybe you are. But if you insist that the answer is the one that will get rid of the luggage for you - then yes, you too can rejoice.

If you feel that you can't come up with an answer, you may need more time, or you may need to talk to someone in order to help out. But you too can rejoice as well, because you're on your way to letting go of the burdens that are holding you back.

<u>Step 5:</u> Travel to the airport, with the paper from step 2, and place said paper in the trash bins marked 'hazardous materials.' Just don't attract too much attention to yourself while doing so (especially not from the airport security guys). On second thought, you could just put it through a shredder or torch it. As long as it's forever gone, you did it. You have rid yourself of that baggage and will aspire to travel light from this day.

That was then. This is now. Okay, I'll stop saying that.

18

The

"My life is a shoe commercial"

Queen

I wanted to name the title for this chapter, *Feel the fear, but do it anyways!* But I hear it's been taken by a different 'self-help' queen. So, I came up with a different moniker. People ask me what is your motto or favorite inspirational quote all the time. Certainly, there are many that have influenced me - definitely specific verses from the Quran and sayings of the Prophet Muhammad, peace be upon him, have (hopefully) shaped who I am. But oddly enough, when I get this question, all I can think of are running shoe slogans. "Just do it!"

"Just do it!" rings in my head whenever I have a task that needs to get done by a specific date, or a meal that needs to be cooked by a specific hour, or if I'm running from a grizzly bear that's chasing me through the forest. Okay, I wasn't actually ever chased by a bear, but you better believe that my first instinct would be to "just run!" Hopefully, I'll be wearing some nice running shoes too.

Without a doubt, the number one thing that will stop you from achieving all that you seek to achieve as you release your inner queen of Sheba is that you don't 'just do it'. If you aren't doing it, then you simply aren't doing it. And I don't care how many self-help books you read, or professionals you hire, or how much more research you need to gather or people you need to convince, or questions you need to ask, there will come a point when you simply must "do it." So, why wait? Just do it. *Now.*

Yes, there may be issues that need to be resolved, people that need to be consulted, or research that needs to be done. So, what's stopping you from doing it? The bear analogy is such a relevant one because if you were to imagine that you were being chased - would you need to ask yourself any questions, or consult with people on the best course of action? If you were to take the time and research it, you may find that the best course of action is not to run, but rather to play dead. But by the time you completed the research, you probably would be dead. In that case, "just running" would have been the better option.

You must keep moving forward, you can't remain glued to your spot, stagnant. You must pursue. After all, isn't life one big marathon?

You know where to start. You are aware of your purpose, know your goals and how to pursue them. You've dealt with the limiting beliefs and baggage that's held you back in the past. Now, you should be spurred to action. You should know that the only way you'll be able to go full force with this is if you simply GO full force with this. How do you do it? How would you learn to swim?

To learn to swim, you might read about learning to swim. You could be inspired by other great swimmers. You might even be able to take online classes to teach you how. But at some point, you're going to have to take the plunge and get into that swimming pool. Eventually, you will have to get into the water.

So, now you're standing on the edge of the pool. Do you put one toe in a time? You could, but that might take long, and swimming classes are usually an hourly expense. Do you stand there waiting for the 'perfect' moment? Ditto on the whole hourly expense thing. Do you need someone to push you in? Believe me when I tell you (from a traumatic personal experience point of view) that this is not a good technique.

No, the best way is to just take the plunge. The water might be cold, but your body will adjust. You might be afraid, but how long have you let the fear stop you? And fear, my dear sisters, is the silliest thing when it comes to pursuing our goals. Unless your fear is based on the fact that your goals will anger Allah - then they have no basis. I hear about fears all the time, and indeed the list of them is endless. Common ones are the fear of failure or success, the fear of losing someone or gaining weight or the fear of wasting time on something doomed to fail.

This last one really gets to me because if you are not "doing" it, believe me, you are wasting your time. You can't wait for the right moment to come by, or for someone else to give you a push. When it comes to making your dreams come true, achieving your life goals and purpose, you simply have to feel the fear, and do it anyway. *Just do it.*

"And say: Work; so Allah will see your work and (so will) His Messenger and the believers; and you shall be brought back to the Knower of the unseen and the seen, then He will inform you of what you used to do." (Quran 9:105)

Allah doesn't look at the result of our actions. He looks at our actions, our work. Even the Prophet Muhammad, peace be upon him, was clearly absolved from responsibility for the actions of his people, whether they chose to become Muslims or not. His task was merely to convey the message. And so if we take this into account when it comes to our goals, and we are able to detach from the outcomes of our actions - wouldn't we be more likely to just follow through and 'do it'? We would know that we don't have to be afraid. We would do it before it is too late, and we are left with the regrets about the things we didn't do.

Now, go put on your running shoes.

Protocol 18

What would you do if fear wasn't a factor? What incredible thing that you do would you like to brag to Allah about? So, when are you going to do it?

If you answered with a resounding "NOW," then that is the right answer. If not, ask why not?

If you still need a friendly push, then you'll want to follow through with this protocol.

Remember some protocols ago, in the chapter titled: *Is that Wonder Woman pretending to be the queen of Sheba?* when you were asked to initiate your 'alter-ego' (so to speak)? Well, this one is the same idea, but different.

As you are about to take action on something you fear or have been procrastinating, picture someone who would so be your cheerleader, someone who would be beaming with pride/gratitude/wonder/amazement   (and   any   or all INCREDIBLE emotions you can think of) if said cheerleader were to witness you taking this action. For your person, you can pick a relative, a mentor, or a historical figure. Maybe you'll choose a child or a childhood friend. I've often written about my childhood friend, Fatimah, who died from cancer before she hit sixteen. Her memory resonates with me constantly as a sign to take action and live in the moment. And her generous spirit, I know, would have made for one enthusiastic cheerleader.

So before you take action, picture your person standing by your side, holding your hand, a solid presence that won't judge you - only love and support you. Let yourself completely surrender to the feeling of knowing that he/she will be there - no matter what. They just want you to do it! Hear their words of encouragement. Hear mine.

You are not alone! We're all in this together! Doing it.

19

Measured to...

fit for a queen

Do not confuse motion and progress. A rocking horse keeps moving but does not make any progress.
-Alfred A. Montapert

𝔐y grandmother, may Allah have mercy on her soul, was a seamstress extraordinaire. In most of my memories of her, she is bent over fine materials, meticulously weaving her needle and thread with the precision of a surgeon. Her specialty was wedding gowns and she was renowned for her craft, not just amongst family and friends, but also to some of the most wealthy and influential people in Egypt and Europe (or at least their wives). Her stunning designs, attention to detail, and dedication to excellence was unprecedented and likely the reasons why she maintained such an elite clientele.

The ladies she tailored the gowns for would come in for 'ajustement' after 'ajustement' (many peppered their Arabic to show off their French), or fittings that stressed the importance of her incredibly high standards. Between adjustments, my grandmother would put a dress away, refusing to work on it until its owner came in and tried it on. As a young girl, it was fascinating for me to see the final product, always true works of art, but the lengthy process seemed to take so long, it was almost unbearable. I could barely wait, and would ask why she just didn't keep going? Why did she have to wait for the fitting results? Even the ladies would urge her to continue on, saying that the constant appointments weren't necessary, that they trusted her to produce perfection.

But she insisted. There would be no further progress on a gown until the bride came in for the fittings my grandmother requested. It was her way. She didn't know shortcuts. And she had the experience and foresight that went beyond the impatience of a young girl or an anxious bride. Oftentimes, the fittings would mean more work for her, seams would have to be taken in or out and alterations could be hazardous to the pattern or the beading. But the end result was always breathtaking. Her masterpieces are still being passed down through the generations.

I often wondered how she kept going, even into her seventies, physically frail and after illness had depleted her. Day in and day out, stitch after stitch, *ajustement* after *ajustement*, she kept on. Have you ever tried producing a wedding gown? If you've attempted to purchase a higher end one, and found the prices shocking, it's likely so because of the sheer amount of physical labor that is put in and the delicate handiwork involved.

How did she do it? She was a testament to the power of motivation. And I think she can teach aspiring queens of Sheba a thing or two on the subject; specifically how to stay the course, and how to keep at it. From my recollection (and a few well documented success principles), my grandmother did it by:

1. Keeping the end in mind. Have a clear picture in your head of what you want to have happen, what you're working towards. My grandmother's sewing room (and much of her home) was storage space for literally hundreds of sewing magazines with full glossy pictures. Her favorite was the German one *Burda* and sometimes I thought she kept them just so I could happily pour over them in all hours of the night. A young girl and fashion magazines can be a lethal combination. But I digress. The point is that my grandmother knew how the end gown would look like when it was finally complete. She knew it because she'd seen it. It's why she could do a fitting and know precisely whether she was moving towards the precious end product or not.

2. Remaining focused. When you have committed to doing something, have made it a priority, and are actively working towards attaining it, make sure that you aren't distracted from the goal at hand. Fight off any temptation to jump to something else or to juggle too much at one time. My grandmother understood this well. Sewing was her thing. She didn't much know how to cook or clean- and if she was working on getting to a certain point with a gown, there was no way she would put it down until she felt that she'd accomplished what needed to be accomplished for that particular sitting. Of course, she had her rules. No sewing on Fridays was the big one. She'd heard a sheikh say that working on Fridays was forbidden in Islam, and she wouldn't budge when others tried to clarify that it was only during the Friday prayer times. But honestly, she needed the rest. And if you're diligently following the 'it's good to be queen' protocol, then you know that she certainly needed this time. And if I told you that her favorite gifts to give to others were warm, velvety blankets and fine chocolates, would you believe me? I kid you not. Indeed, the things we inherit from our mothers and grandmothers.

3. Measuring. Ajustement. Measuring. Ajustement. This is perhaps the most critical point of all, because indeed "that which is measured improves." Obviously, for a seamstress, the likelihood of how well the dress fits its intended owner is the epitome of whether it's a success or not. And the progress from yards of fabric to picturesque gown is something that is visually tangible. You can literally see the progress. But for some of our goals, that might not be the case. We become haphazard and we don't measure progress that we can't see. Unfortunately, this sometimes makes us give up. If my grandmother had one dress that wasn't working out - how would she know this? She'd see it by measuring. Then she'd have to decide if she could make the necessary adjustments or if she'd have to go back to the drawing board. The gown must go on.

The concept of measuring in coaching principles is a highly touted one. In its most simplest of forms, the life wheel gives a quick bird's eye view of how you are doing in the slices of your life. To create your own life wheel, you can draw a circle and divide it into eight equal slices. For each slice, you name a category of your life - emotions, career, spirituality, marriage, health, social connections, family are common ones. Of course, you can make 6 slices instead of 8, and you can pick and choose, add or delete the slices that are relevant to you at this point in your life. The eight I've mentioned are guidelines, albeit, commonly chosen as the categories most relevant to people's lives.

Every week (or two - or whatever measurement cycle works best for you) you rate the categories on a scale of 1 to 10, with 1 being the worst, 10 being the best (or the other way around if you please). As the weeks progress and you continue to measure, you can see what areas you're improving in and what areas you need to work on. Of course, you'd first need to get a feel of what the numbers mean to you. What would a ten look like in each category? How about a one? Not to try to put ideas in your head, but for demonstration purposes – let's look at the marriage category. One sister might say, "I know my marriage would be a ten if my husband whisked me off to Paris every six months for a romantic getaway and bought me roses and fine chocolates at least once a week." Okay. Another sister might say, "I know my marriage would be a ten if my husband would pick up after himself and actually run a load of laundry." Okay. I know what you're wondering - which one is more spot on? Well, I'll save the marriage discussion for another time. Or another book.

Just know here that value expectations will vary from woman to woman, and only you can decide what your best scores look like. And only you can realize what's working and what isn't so that you know how to move forward.

That which is measured improves.

Protocol 19

This is where math class comes in handy. It is also where you're going to start coming up with your own protocols. Above, I've described the life wheel, but I haven't (purposely) placed it as the protocol. This is because you can take the same idea and apply it in any number of ways.

You can measure your budget, for instance, with an online calculator. You can use a graph to chart optimal health scores, like blood pressure. You can ask your friends to periodically fill out a survey to determine how much fun you are to be around. But you don't have to go that far. So long as you are measuring what matters to you and your goals, you'll be fine.

What method will work for you when it comes to measuring? Take out your journals and decide what you'll be measuring, how you'll be measuring it, and how often will you measure it?

It is entirely up to you, and you don't have to go all high-tech here using the latest business software (I've actually seen that done). Of course, it you wanted to use Quicken to measure your marriage, you could I guess. But if you're anything like me, a few fingers and maybe a good calculator are the most you'll need. I hate numbers, I hate numbers - sorry, I love numbers, I love numbers. That's what I have to keep repeating.

Like I said, this is where math class comes in handy.

20

Time after Time

$\mathcal{S}$eventy-two hours is all you have. I once heard that there is a seventy two hour time window for people to truly start implementing something new after they first hear it. This makes sense when you consider all the 'jump start' diets that fizzle within the first couple of days, or the energy boost when we decide we're going to take on a challenge we're eager about only to falter within the first few hours. How easily do we make excuses for not trying and how easily do we give up? How many New Year's Resolutions are broken before the month ends? It's always something I'm afraid of during live seminars where the women leave so full of energy - so ready and inspired to release their inner queen of Sheba. They have taken notes - maybe even gotten some handouts. And things look good, but I wonder if it is enough. I warn them that they have that limited time frame, but I wonder if I have cramped too much in the seminar, will they go home and not know where to start? Will they then give up?

This is actually why I felt like the book should take precedence, because it will be that constant companion that women need. As long as it's not collecting dust on a shelf, women would only ever be seventy two hours away from being their own best life coach.

And if a time problem persists, it's likely to be one of the following:

A. Perhaps we may feel like the time isn't right, that there is just too much going on.

B. Perhaps we need some time-management skills.

While both A and B might seem similar, but they are two different issues altogether. In the first, we know what we should be doing, we rationally understand it, but for some reason, we just aren't doing it. In the second, we literally feel like we don't have the time - and we need some techniques to get that one resolved.

The good news is that in this chapter, both A and B will be resolved, and you can get on with releasing your inner queen of Sheba within the time window of seventy-two hours. If you are reading here now and you've been doing great things so much so that you can't be stopped, then I honor you. May Allah grant you much success in every category of your life and may this process continue to be incredible and inspiring for you.

If you have yet to start applying the protocols, then consider this chapter added incentive to do so now. And I'm certain that you'll do better on your journey because of it. Finally, if you've been doing the protocols, but need to kick it up a notch, to challenge yourself with a BANG! then consider this chapter your chance to up the ante.

Part A

You have the right intentions, know what you should be doing, but you've stopped. To get going, you need to recognize that:

1) **Talk is Cheap.** Too much talk is also known as the killer of all actions. Consider the diet that we endlessly talk to our sisters about starting. Consider the strategy-planning we do when working on the next big business idea that we subsequently lose interest in. Hopefully, from previous chapters, you have learned to embrace the 'my life is a shoe-commercial' attitude and will keep doing.

Just do it + stop talking about doing it = a highly effective queen of Sheba. Now just do it. You have 72 hours. Implement it now because the clock is ticking.

2) **You should be working that tape measure.** I've

known women who like to spend a lot of time dreaming about what their castle in the sky will look like. And while this may be a happy place, it might also signify that you're substituting fluffy dreams for action. If you truly want that castle in the sky to come down to earth, you have to close the gap between the two realms, and keep measuring how far along you're moving in the quest. You have 72 hours to get your head out of the clouds and to implement this knowledge now! The clock is ticking.

3) If there is something standing in your way, make like a queen and yell: "Off with its head!" When it comes to moving forward with our mission, certain things/thoughts/people (or any combination thereof) will support our quest. Others will not. If there's something or someone standing in your way, what are you going to do about it? How will you banish the distraction? Now do it within the next 72 hours.

Part B
Steven Covey, author of bestselling book *The 7 Habits of Highly Effective People*, defined and demonstrated the four quadrants of time management, strategies that have been used by millions, and a success principle that I adopt and encourage others to all the time. It's so good, I've worked into this chapter's protocol. Here's a glorified example to ease your understanding of each time quadrant:

Last night's dinner included Moroccan style chicken with olives and preserved lemons, a side of white rice, and the cuisine's traditional salad known as charmoula. I made it all myself and for dessert, I tried out a recipe for honey cookies with orange blossom water. With my upbringing (my parents ran a few Middle Eastern restaurants) and traditions, you'd think I would love to cook. I don't. Some might say that with all the things I have going on, that cooking for me is a distraction. It isn't. And getting fulfillment from cooking? Please! **rolls eyes **

The truth is, I hate to cook but I do it because I have to. A hungry teenager, a screaming toddler, a husband who doesn't ask for much except that he gets a decent meal once a day, and a couple of more mouths to feed in between would surmount to a full fledged mutiny if there wasn't a meal on the table at 6 pm every night. And so I pull myself away from everything else and head to the kitchen at about 5:45 pm to do what must be done. I supply because there is demand.

In taking ownership of your life and moving forward in achieving your goals, time becomes of the utmost importance. Actions can be taken, mistakes can be corrected, but an hour gone is an hour gone. You can't bring it back. And many find that all of a sudden, there just aren't enough of them in a day to get all that you want done. You want to get your business off the ground, make sure that you are maintaining your Quran memorization, go to the gym, get your daughter to school, eat - and don't forget sleep.

Feeling overwhelmed? Enter the "time zone". This should help you channel your energies into the things that really matter so that you can be an expert in time management. To categorize the tasks in your life according to the time you take to achieve them, here are Steven Covey's 4 quadrants with their AKA (also known as) aliases:

- QI - Important and Urgent : Demand
- QII - Important but Not Urgent : Fulfillment
- QIII - Not Important but Urgent: Delusion
- QIV - Not Important and Not Urgent: Distraction

Got 72 hours? Let's do it!

Protocol 20

In the protocol, you will first have to take a look at your current schedule. If you aren't sure how your day is going down - take a few days and log it all. Ask yourself where the activities you're currently participating in belong in relation to the category. So, for example, are you really that tired, or is the extra time you spend napping some sort of distraction? Is it possible that your constant checking and replying to your emails a form of delusion? Are all your replies that urgent? What would really happen if you checked once a day instead of ten? What are these tasks a substitute for? These are the ones you may need to call the bluff on, the ones that fit into the quadrant labeled delusion.

In terms of demand, this is where my cooking task fits in. What are your must dos? These are the things that if you didn't do them, all-chaos-would-break-loose-and-you'll-be-in-a-pile-of-rubbish type things. Make sure to find a way to do them in the most efficient manner as possible.

Finally, in the fulfillment category, you'll find tasks that aren't urgent, but important. These are the things that will give you inner contentment and satisfaction, the things that will bring purpose to your life. Reading Quran, buying a gift for your mother, playing with your child, or visiting a sick friend are examples of tasks that have a place here.

After you've analyzed your schedule and fit your tasks into the appropriate areas, this is the process you need to follow in order to maximize your time:

1. Plan to do tasks which are important and urgent first.
2. Fit the urgent, but not important ones in next. But remember, to really analyze the things that fall into this category.
3. Put time aside when you will do the not urgent, but

important tasks.

4. Know time wasters and go all "cut off their head" on them; resolve to eliminate these tasks from your schedule.

By identifying the root cause of that which wastes our time, we can take back our hours and ultimately our productivity. We'll be able to finish what we start, and rid ourselves of the feelings of being overwhelmed and at a loss for time. We'll be able to quickly figure out what few actions will give us the most results, and we'll have more time to be fulfilled.

Are you ready to apply this protocol in your life?

May Allah bless all your time.

21

The castle

that

happiness built

As I write this last chapter, I can honestly say, that I'm feeling a sense of happiness unlike anything I've felt before. And I've had many happy moments before, thankfully. It was a happy moment that led me to write this book, and many thousand happy moments that I experienced during the process. And I think that it may have been the pursuit of happiness that led you to it in the first place. So, happy, is certainly the operative word here. That's what we seek, all humans. It's the common denominator sought by the millionaire in his private jet closing a lucrative business deal, or the young woman enjoying a picnic with her closest friend, or the aspiring queen of Sheba.

No matter what we want or how different or unique our wants are, the underlying objective is the pursuit of happiness. Here's an exercise to prove my point:

Step One: I want you to think of 3 things that you really, really, want. List them here:

1.

2.

3.

Good stuff! Now, look back at that list and think about what it is that you're *really after*.

Step Two: Without fail, when people list the physical or material things that they want - it's not the actual thing that they want, but it's the feeling that is associated with the particular item. Next, please answer:

When I have (item 1):
I will feel _____and I will feel _____and I will feel ____

When I have (item 2):
I will feel _____and I will feel _____and I will feel ____

When I have (item 3):
I will feel _____and I will feel _____and I will feel ____

If you're like most people, the word 'happy' should have come in first or second, or definitely third. And if that was the case, you were just saving the best for last. Here's one sister's response who knew what was happening and tried to resist the word (but it eventually came out),
"When I have a pious husband, I will feel like I've fulfilled my duties in Islam. Fulfilling my duties in Islam will make me feel like Allah is pleased with me. And when Allah is pleased with me, I will feel happy."

The pursuit of happiness underlines so many things. Other books (besides this one) have been written, stories have been shared, movies have been made, and when you factor in all the things we do in each day, the list is literally endless. It has been my hope that everything in this book has moved towards giving you this too, making you recognize what, in your heart you know, will give you happiness. Releasing you inner queen of Sheba has been about defining the purpose and goals that will move you towards that happiness. And it has been about the techniques that should allow you to embrace it in each moment. In this last chapter, you'll learn how to forever keep the "happiness habit" alive and well.

So, what are the practices of happy people? Many have been studied, tested, and documented, but here are my favorite four:

1. They continually strive to find their most authentic self. If you were to paint a picture of happiness on earth - what would it look like? Would you be sitting in a peaceful place contemplating the magnitude and splendor of Allah's creation? People the world over will answer that indeed peaceful contentment in a pleasurable place would be the setting for their happiness paintings. Truly, this is a big part of happiness, but, there is more to it. To arrive at that happy place, people need to have a higher purpose, to use their unique talents to work toward their own personal growth and be actually doing what makes them feel connected to that happiness painting. One woman paints a picture of herself in a valley of flowers, with a pen and paper, writing words that will inspire others to be happy. Another woman's painting has her sitting on the back steps of the orphanage she's helped develop, while she watches the children playing. Still another woman paints a farm with her daughter milking the cows and her son sowing the harvest, and a houseful of family members that she is making lemonade for.

Each woman keeps this happiness painting in their hearts and on their walls to remind them. As they move towards achieving it, they appreciate the moments knowing that they're doing something wonderful. This gives them authentic happiness. Even if it takes forever, or if their painting comes to life today - so long as they're using their most authentic self to get there, they're good.

2. They rig their lives to allow happiness in. Sisters who've established a routine that makes them happy understand that they must make the time (the fulfillment category) to continually allow for the happiness to come in. A morning cup of coffee that's more like a ritual, a workout in the gym that can't be missed, avoiding a co-worker that really infuriates, or a period one day of the week just to snuggle under a warm blanket gossiping with your mother are examples of rigging that is meant to produce happiness and contentment. By enjoying moments in this way, happy people are more conscious and tolerant of harder moments so that the happier ones will continually supersede.

3. They give themselves permission to be happy. As much as we women are the nurturers, as much as we take care of others and are everything to everybody *is* as much as we need to focus on our own spiritual growth and contentment. We need to forgive ourselves and approach ourselves from a place of tolerance and understanding, and happiness. And when we are in tune to our happiness, we are more able and ready to fulfill the nurturing roles for others. Happy people are more open to helping others than anyone else. Happy people do make better mothers, wives, daughters, entrepreneurs, and definitely queens of Sheba.

4. They know gratitude. To appreciate each moment is to be grateful to Allah for it. To thank those we love who have allowed us the moment is to thank Allah. To recognize that each moment is precious because the experience of it allows you to mature is to know gratitude. When the moments are hard or overwhelming or even mindless, stepping back and listening to the lesson each moment is trying to teach you, is to know gratitude. Indeed, to savor each moment in the pursuit of releasing your inner queen of Sheba is to know gratitude.

To finally be able to offer you (my dear sister) this (book) and to come to the end of the journey is to know gratitude. All praise is due to Allah, the most beneficial, the most merciful.

This is my moment of happiness.

Protocol 21

Paint your happiness scene. Or make a collage filled with the photos (online images, magazines, or personal collection) of the things and dreams you want to accomplish. Put this vision up on your wall, the one you spend the most time looking at. Take two pictures of the vision and keep one in your purse (or wherever else, remember "whatever works for you will work for you") so that you can carry your happiness at all times. Put the other picture on the cover of your journal so that as you continually chronicle the moments, you'll know why you are doing so.

That's it. Now, go be happy.

Let us eat Cake
By way of Farewell

How have you benefitted from this journey?

For me, this journey has been lonely at times. I was literally holed up by my computer for almost a year working on it each evening until the wee hours of the morning, but I'm not complaining because it has been such an incredible one too. I've met so many fabulous sisters who immediately understood the concept and became part of the team. Along with the slight caffeine addiction I developed, it was their encouragement that fueled me - and the fact that this would soon be ready to share. "We need this, Heba," I heard often, and felt blessed knowing that I could in some small way, serve. This is my gift to those sisters, and to you, my sister. I hope to meet you in person soon, but if it doesn't happen in this life, I'm praying that we are sisters in the next. Keep me in your prayers as you are in mine.

I pray that you've gone through this and realized that you are a daughter of great women – that you can stand on their shoulders and know that you are able to lead your life, just as they were able to lead theirs. I pray that you have gained a greater understanding and confidence of who you are and how you'd like to live so that you can always focus on your abilities and utilize your unique gifts. I pray that you have expanded your definition of what is possible, that you look to the future with hope and enthusiasm and trust that you will be able to find great happiness. I pray that you become the beacon for others, a shining example of strength and character and brilliant achievement. I pray that your legacy will have the makings of one that proves to be a medium for the betterment of your family, your community, and your society. I pray that the world will be a better place because you lived on it. And I pray that you get your castle in the next life as well.

Allah sets forth an example for those who believe — the wife of Pharaoh (Asiyah) who said, "My Lord, build for me with Thee a home in paradise..." (Quran 66:11)

You did well. Now, plate yourself a slice of cake (you can have an extra one for me), and keep doing well, dear queen of Sheba.